THE BALLET COMPANION

Other books by Walter Terry

THE
$\mathcal{B}$allet $\mathcal{C}$ompanion

A POPULAR GUIDE FOR THE BALLET-GOER

by Walter Terry

Illustrated with drawings by MEL JUAN
and photographs

DODD, MEAD & COMPANY, NEW YORK

Library of Congress Catalog Card Number: 67-26148

Printed in the United States of America
by The Cornwall Press, Inc., Cornwall, N. Y.

2-0930

For Emily Coleman, my dearest companion
at the theater of dance in our seats "two on the aisle"

Acknowledgments

My gratitude to Genevieve Oswald and every member of her staff in the Dance Collection of the New York Public Library for swift and accurate assistance in research details and in supplying rare illustrations; to Jacqueline Maskey for her invaluable aid in helping me update the listing of ballet productions, in preparing the index, and in proofreading; to the dancers, choreographers, composers, designers and dance followers who shared dance thoughts with me; and to the late Lillian Moore, America's foremost dance historian, a teacher and a critic, who was, for more than a quarter of a century, a continuing source of knowledge and inspiration to me and to all of us who write about the act and the art of dancing.

W.T.

Contents

for ballet. Dances and ballets created to music written for non-theater use.

4. *The Designer*   106

Styles in designs and costumes for the extravaganzas of Catherine de Medici, Louis XIV, subsequent monarchs and courts. Styles for period when Greek-Roman myths were bases of ballets. Changes in designs when ballet shifted to Romantic Age. Design today.

5. *Ballet Dress*   122

How tights and tutus came into being. The introduction of the toe shoe into ballet. Crowns, coronets, and wigs.

6. *Ballet Training*   135

Finding a good school and teacher. At what age to begin. Different exercises for boys and girls. Number of lessons per week. Where and how the professional dancer studies, trains, and is coached in techniques, period styles, roles, etc.

7. *Interpretation and Individuality*   155

How the ballerina and danseur differentiate between characterizations and performing styles of different periods, countries, choreographers. The art of partnering.

8. *Injuries, Accidents and Laughs*   172

How accidents occur. Daily disciplines. Miscalculations on stage.

Illustrations

DRAWINGS

THE BALLET COMPANION

Chapter 1

Ballet: Its Origins and Meanings

Ballet is a theatrical trinity, for the word itself has three distinct, though related, meanings. "Ballet" is a technique, a system of dance movement different from all other dance techniques. "Ballet" is also a company, a troupe of men and women who perform before audiences and who utilize the technique of ballet in their performing. "Ballet" signifies, in its third definition, a production, a theatrical work in one or more acts which communicates ideas, be they stories or abstract patterns, through dance. When we "go to the ballet," then, we are seeing this theatrical trinity in action: we are witnessing a ballet company using ballet technique in a ballet production.

Ballet, a word which has its roots in the Italian "ballare" (to dance)—and today's "ballroom" is a place in which to dance—had its beginnings in Italy almost five centuries ago. The technique would not be recognizable to us as ballet; the performances were actually occasions, and the participants were nobles and courtiers.

Even before Columbus set sail for the unknown New World, the ducal courts of Italy were celebrating special occasions—betrothals, marriages, visits by heads of state—through elaborate banquet-fêtes which included declamation, dancing, music, pageantry and scenic effects. The dancing? It was simply the court dances of the day incorporated into the plan of the spectacle. Ballet technique as we know it had not yet emerged, but its source was to be these very court dances, and the "plan" of a banquet-fête heralded the day when a choreographer, who might be described as a creative planner, would arrange dances and pantomime and music and settings and, of course, fuse them into an entity which would be called a ballet.

The stories used at these banquet-balls were classical, derived from Greek and Roman myths. The visiting dignitary might be compared thereby to a hero of antiquity, or even a god, and certainly a princely couple about to be wed would find their counterparts in lovely legends. The banquet itself was an integral part of the concept of these pre-ballet events. Naturally, Neptune and his attendants from the sea were summoned for the fish course, and who but Diana, the goddess of the hunt, would preside when venison was served? Wine? Ah, Bacchus.

The popularity of these spectacles spread, and when Catherine de Medici became Queen of France, she brought to the French court the Italian's fondness for dancing and dance entertainments. The Queen herself was said to be an excellent dancer, but she was also a producer of ballet, and it was in this capacity that she presided over a historic moment in the development of the dance art.

By her command, on October 15, 1581, the *Ballet Comique*

de la Reine, usually considered to be the first real ballet, was given. Ten thousand royal guests saw this ballet spectacle which lasted for five hours. Its cost staggered the French treasury. The choreographer, Beaujoyeulx, who was of Italian origin, based his ballet on the myth of Circe. Not all was dancing. There were verses spoken, elaborate scenery and costumes displayed, and even mechanical effects were employed in creating spectacular arrivals and departures and transformations.

The *Ballet Comique de la Reine* was commissioned in order to celebrate a royal betrothal, and its cast was composed of royal and noble ladies and gentlemen (the ballet had not yet established a school for professional dancers), but its impact was greater than that normally attendant upon a lavish social occasion. Here, in fact, was a new concept of dance theater, for these were not the isolated divertissements and scenes of the Italian banquet-fêtes but, rather, a theater work with a continuously developed theme, with a beginning, middle and an end, with choreographic disciplines making it a dramatic entity.

Such was the success of this "first" ballet that ambassadors and envoys from other lands hastened to inform their sovereigns of Catherine's remarkable achievement; and in the years which followed, the courts of Europe, giving new respect to dancing masters, endeavored to emulate the enviable glitter and originality which the Queen of France had achieved. The concept of ballet was developing and spreading.

The beginnings of the ballet art should by no means be considered synonymous with the beginnings of the dance art; ballet is simply one aspect of the most ancient of art expressions, dance. When Beaujoyeulx choreographed the *Ballet Comique*, the classical dance of India, an ethnic form called Bharata Natyam, with an elaborate movement technique, highly distinctive style, and a vast array of thematic material at its disposal, was already two thousand years old. Other peoples and other nations had long since developed their own, their ethnic dance arts. But ballet was to be different. It was to be not the manifestation of one culture, one heritage, one race, and it was to be nurtured not by France alone but by other countries—Denmark, Russia, Austria, England, America—and it was to belong to the entire world.

But it was a baby in the annals of dance. Not only could various cultures date their dance art in terms of thousands of years, but the act of dancing itself could be outlined in millennia. Dance, very probably man's first form of art expression (preceding music and poetry and drama), was older than man himself: the courtship dances of birds and animals, now fully documented and recorded on movie film, attest to this. And ballet is a late offshoot of this compulsion to express oneself in rhythmic, ordered, meaningful movement... in dance.

For a long time after Catherine de Medici, ballet was principally "at the pleasure" of the court. This imposed limitations on the new art since courtiers and even kings, though submitting to dance instruction, had neither the time nor the inclination to devote hours a day to improving and extending a dance technique. It also imposed a style, a behavior, which exists to this day. Deportment in classical ballet is elegant because ballet was invented by aristocrats; today's ballet bow, the *grand révérence*, echoes the formal obeisance to Louis

En Révérence

XIV, the Sun King himself, Apollo reincarnated, the "danseur extraordinaire."

Not only was the style of ballet colored by its courtly origins, but its technique was similarly determined. The polished floors of palaces invited the slide and the glide; the dress of royal personages governed the way the dancer would step, would gesture, would raise his arms or hold his spine.

Positions of Feet

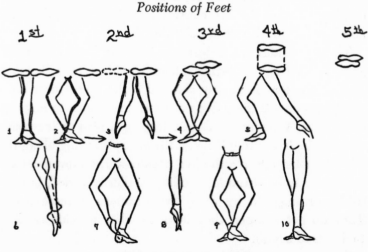

Glissade Jeté—Assemblé

Furthermore, the popular court dances—the stately pavane, the quiet sarabande, the lively galliard, the joyous gigue— would give their simple steps to the choreographer who would transform a glide into a *glissade,* a modest jump into a striking *jeté,* a pause into a *posé,* a chain of simple ballroom steps into an *enchaînement* of virtuosic action which would dazzle the world.

The culmination of ballet growth for the sixteenth century was most certainly represented by the resplendent *Ballet Comique de la Reine,* but a more modest and immensely important contribution to the development of ballet was to be found in a book. This book was called *Orchésographie* and was published in 1588, just a few years after the *Ballet Comique.* Its author was a priest, Thoinot Arbeau, and the book described the dances, along with musical notes, popular during that century. Here, the turnout of the legs and feet was recorded, and this, of course, heralded the establishment, a century later, of the five classical positions of the feet, the absolute technical base of ballet itself.

These positions are so designed that the dancer can move easily to the front, to the back, to either side or on a diagonal. And to this day, in strictly classical ballet, the dancer *must* start from one of these five positions and return to any one of the five. Whether he does a leap or a turn or leg-beats, whether he is vaulting through the air or traveling along the floor, he must observe the five positions. His movement excursions may be virtuosic, dazzling, endlessly varied, but the discipline imposed by these five positions is inescapable. They do not hamper, they help, for they provide controls to flights of action.

There are comparable positions of the arms (called *port*

de bras), combined with related positions of the head and inclinations (directional) of the body.

These basic positions have been in force in classical ballet for more than three centuries. They are not in force, of course, for those national dances—the jota, the czardas, etc.

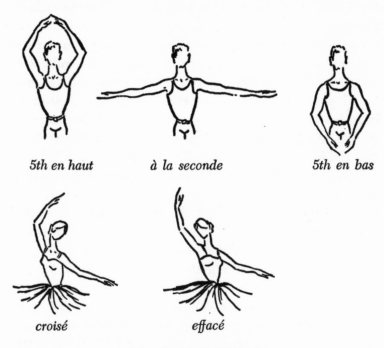

5th en haut   à la seconde   5th en bas

croisé   effacé

ARM AND BODY POSITIONS

—which have been incorporated into the general action of a ballet, nor are they required of the character dancer—one who plays a witch, for example, or the Wolf in *Little Red Riding Hood*—but in all classical variations or measures performed by the ballerina, the danseur, the soloists and the corps de ballet, the basic positions are always observed.

For example, Odette, the Queen of the Swans in *Swan Lake*, may move her head as if she were preening or move her arms in a way indicative of fluttering wings, but the arms will start from a basic position and conclude with one, and the feet will observe their traditional positions. Odile (the Black Swan), when she comes to that part of the coda of the third-act pas de deux where she is required to execute the sequence of thirty-two fouettés (whipping turns on one leg), usually starts out from fourth position (it is a wide, solid and firm base, the strongest stance in ballet), and she ends in fifth position as she concludes the electrifying fouettés; her body has become a human top and she thus culminates the section in the narrowest, tightest, most closed-in position that the feet can achieve in ballet, fifth position.

Three hundred years ago, there were no fouettés, no multiple pirouettes on *pointe* (dancing on toe did not come into use until toward the close of the eighteenth century) and few of the virtuosities we know today. But the positions of the feet had been established, and the technique of the classical dance had begun to be developed.

The year 1661 is the key year in the academic progress of ballet. In that year Louis XIV, King of France and himself a dancer by avocation and interested in the arts as a whole, commanded that the Académie Royale de la Danse be established in Paris. This was to be the institution where teachers of dance would arrange a training program, a ballet curriculum, for students desiring to become truly professional dancers. Ballet, under the auspices of the Crown, had become a vocation for artists dedicating their lives to the theater and not, as theretofore, principally an avocation of the nobility for the amusement of the court.

Under the direction of France's leading composer, Jean Baptiste Lully, the Royal Academy flourished and, in 1681, produced the world's first professional ballerina, Lafontaine. Before her, ladies of the court appeared in court ballets, but in the theater itself, female roles were performed by young boys. Although by the time Lafontaine had made her debut, Pierre Beauchamp, the ballet master at the Academy, had inaugurated a training program which firmly established the use of the five positions of the feet, the essential turnout of the limbs (ultimately to reach a ninety-degree angle) and

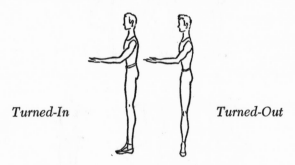

Turned-In   *Turned-Out*

the posture of the dancer, Lafontaine herself resembled not at all the ballerina of today. It is doubtful if we would have recognized her as one.

She wore shoes with heels, cumbersome dress which reached to the ground and towering headdresses. It is a minor miracle that she could move. But move she did and her dancing had Paris at her feet. The steps were still pretty much those of the court social dances, but they were now beginning to be exaggerated, exploited and refined. The men dancers, less confined by heavy dress and with freedom of the legs, had passed the female dancers technically, for they were already doing pirouettes and leaving the ground for aerial steps (something the ladies could not do, fashions in dress being what they were).

But now progress was to become swift in matters of technique. Françoise Prévost, who succeeded Lafontaine as pre-

Pirouette—en dehors

miere danseuse at the opera, dressed rather like her predecessor, but she added to the dancer's scope in terms of mime, of gesture, of acting related to dance. But Prévost's successors, Marie Camargo and Marie Sallé, were true revolutionaries.

Camargo, sometimes credited with inventing the *entrechat* (it is more likely that she was the first female dancer to

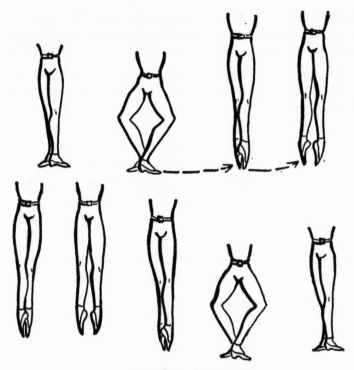

Entrechat—Quatre

execute it), transformed the ballerina from a terre-à-terre dancer, that is, one who moves on the ground, into an aerial creature. Perhaps inspired by the leaps, beats and turns of one of her teachers, the celebrated danseur Blondi, Camargo shed her heels (which gave her a much better spring) and shortened her skirt (to give her greater freedom of movement). It is also possible that she was the first danseuse to achieve the ninety-degree turnout essential to the fullest mobility (and maneuverability) of the ballet dancer.

Sallé was very different. She was not especially interested

in steps nor in physical virtuosity. Her concern was with the
meaningfulness of movement, the drama inherent in dance.
She was the first female choreographer in the field of ballet,
and her major creation was *Pygmalion,* which made use of
her skills as an actress-dancer (later, she even essayed the
title role in her own ballet version of Shakespeare's *Hamlet*).
Sallé was also a revolutionary in costume for dance. She did
away, in her *Pygmalion,* with the heavy skirts and panniers,
and selected draped dresses. She replaced elaborate hair ar-
rangements with hair falling loosely and simply in the manner she presumed to be correct for classical Greece.

Both Camargo and Sallé, then, not only left their marks on
the ballet of the early eighteenth century (they were at their
height in the 1720's and 1730's) but also extended the technique and the style of ballet itself.

The ballerinas, of course, were not by any means solely
responsible for the technical development of ballet, although
many of them were important contributors. The danseurs, as
they experimented with new feats of skill, new expositions
of male prowess, most certainly added to ballet's technique.
But the ballet masters, the choreographers, even the ballet
theoreticians, were the ones whose vision required more and
more of the dancers. Progress was made in the classroom but
it was also made in rehearsals for the stage. "Try this. Try
that," the choreographer asked his dancers while in the process of making dances, and in the process of trying out new
ideas, the technique of ballet grew.

In the mid-eighteenth century, Jean Georges Noverre began his career as the most influential choreographer of his
century. There were other major choreographers, of course,
among them Angiolini; but Noverre, through his many

ballets, through his associations with important artists and through his now historic book, *Lettres sur la Danse et sur les Ballets*, became an art revolutionary, a ballet pioneer, a leader and even a pedagogue. His students and those he influenced carried on and extended his principles into the next century. As one who espoused the *ballet d'action*—that is, a ballet in which movements are expressive and are used not merely for technical display but for contributing to the theme, the characters and the progress of the plot—he gave the art of ballet a balance it was beginning to lose in the mad rush for increasing physical skills without thought of dramatic point and purpose.

Gaetan Vestris, the greatest male dancer of his generation (during the middle of the eighteenth century) and his son, Auguste Vestris, whom his father referred to as the "God of the Dance," the greatest male dancer of his generation, both extended the technical accomplishments of the male dancer while not neglecting the expressive side of ballet. Gaetan, in fact, danced for Noverre and proved himself to be a brilliant mime; and Auguste, along with his dazzling pirouettes and entrechats, developed into a splendid teacher of ballet.

But still other startling changes in ballet were to come as the nineteenth century approached. In the last decade of the 1700's, the female dancer rose briefly onto pointe, onto the very tip of her toes. It lasted only a moment, for the shoes she wore were as soft as gloves, but it heralded a new age of ballet. The age was ushered in by yet another Marie—Marie Taglioni. The scene was Paris, the year was 1832 and the ballet created especially for her by her father (Philippe Taglioni) was *La Sylphide*.

The male dancers—the Vestrises and all—moved into the

background (where they would stay for nearly a century) as the ballerina moved up onto the delicate, perilous pointe. The old ballet themes, those taken from Greek and Roman myths, were gone as the Romantic Age swept in. The ballerina, in roles as sylphs, sprites, fairies and creatures of fancy, became the enchanting but elusive female. Her pointe was almost her pedestal at which mere mortal man came to worship.

La Sylphide is the story of a Scottish youth who is betrothed to a village girl whom he loves dearly. But as the wedding approaches, a sylphide, white of dress, winged and swift, flies into the room and entrances the young hero. Captivated by her, he follows her to her woodland glade, deserting his bride-to-be. A witch gives him an enchanted scarf with which to catch the sylphide, but it is poisoned, and as he places it around her shouders, she shudders, her wings fall to the floor and she expires. She is borne aloft through the treetops by her attendant sylphs while the Scotsman mourns.

La Sylphide and Taglioni conquered Paris and soon all of Europe. The Danish dancer and Denmark's greatest choreographer, Auguste Bournonville, a pupil of Auguste Vestris, returned to Copenhagen in 1836 where he staged *La Sylphide* for another great ballerina, the Danish Lucile Grahn, and although the Taglioni *Sylphide* has long since been forgotten, the Danish version has remained in the Royal Danish Ballet's active repertory ever since its premiere.

Taglioni was not without rivals. Her nearest was the earthy, fiery Viennese Fanny Elssler, and the Paris public was fairly evenly divided between the Taglionistes, who worshipped the pure, delicate, ethereal Marie, and the Elsslerites, who adored their "pagan" goddess. Carlotta Grisi, who seemed to combine the ethereal nature of Taglioni with the earthiness of Elssler, had an opportunity to put her range of interpretation to the test in one of the greatest and certainly the most enduring of the Romantic ballets, *Giselle*, in which she was a mortal peasant maid in Act I, and a Wili, a ghost maiden, in Act II. And ever since Grisi's day, *Giselle*, which is to the ballerina what *Hamlet* is to the actor, has been the challenge and the goal of every classical ballerina.

Mentioning *Giselle* or *La Sylphide* (which is quite a different ballet from Fokine's much later tribute to it, *Les Sylphides*) might lead one to believe that with these ballets the technique of the classical dance had reached its zenith. Not a bit of it. In writing of Taglioni, Elssler, Grisi, Grahn and Fanny Cerrito, the critics used extravagant language, but the "fantastic toe" or the "amazing exertions" to which they referred would probably be neither fantastic nor amazing by our standards today.

The pointe work was certainly limited. In the Age of Taglioni, the ballerina rose onto both pointes, stepped onto one pointe in arabesque (or some other pose) and stirred an audience with a few pas de bourrées (in her very soft slippers). Pirouettes? An enchaînement of traveling turns? They were customarily done on half-toe (in Denmark, until as late as 1950, such steps in the traditional Bournonville ballets were executed on half-toe). But what a vast technical advance since the 1700's!

The advance made itself felt around the world.

The great capitals of Europe—Copenhagen, St. Petersburg, Vienna, London and others—had long delighted in that Italian-born ballet which came to flourish in France. Royal

*Arabesque
sur la Pointe*

Bourrées sur les Pointes

ballets and their academies were founded, and national characteristics and styles extended the range of the art itself as it expanded, geographically, its world horizons. Even distant America had its ballet in Colonial days. English and French dancing masters not only performed in the European manner but also instructed local talent in the most cultured cities of the New World, among them Philadelphia, destined to produce a dazzling array of fine dancers from the late 1700's right into the middle of the twentieth century.

John Durang, a Pennsylvanian, became America's first premier danseur. His popularity—the Durang Hornpipe was something of a trademark—ranged from the general public right up to the Presidency, to George Washington himself.

The coming of the Romantic Age spurred American ballet enterprise onward. It wasn't merely that our shores were visited by Fanny Elssler (in a triumphant tour that caused, among other things, an adjournment of Congress so that the legislators could attend her matinee), by members of the Taglioni family and other celebrated stars of the "new" ballet, but it challenged our own dancers to match the luminaries from abroad.

La Sylphide crossed the ocean. Mary Ann Lee, a Philadelphia ballerina, hustled to Paris to learn *Giselle* and returned to stage a production of her own in America almost on the heels of the Paris premiere. Reversing the order of things, another Philadelphian, Augusta Maywood (once a celebrated child prodigy known as the Little Augusta), crossed the ocean to become the first American ballerina in history to invade the near-sacred halls of the Paris Opera as a premiere danseuse and to win fame in the theaters of Italy itself. American men dancers? Why, who should Elssler select as a partner for American appearances but another Pennsylvanian, George Washington Smith, mustaches and all!

But the Romantic Age, with its idols, its avant-garde approach to ballet and its vastly advanced technique, was destined to grow old. It lived on in Paris and London and Copenhagen, but it lost much of its potency—except, possibly, in Denmark, where the choreographic genius of Bournonville bestowed it with an undying vibrancy—and a new ballet age had to come into being. It came with the Frenchman Marius Petipa, who journeyed to Russia and who made the Russian Imperial Ballet the symbol of the best in ballet anywhere in the world. Indeed, under Petipa, the words "ballet" and "Russian" became almost inseparable. And a generation of work and achievement was needed to remove the Russian monopoly and restore the international stature of ballet.

Nonetheless, Petipa gave the world of ballet new and glorious horizons.

The Age of Petipa saw the technique of ballet develop to undreamed-of accomplishments. The advance in technique was spurred by the ballets which Petipa created during his long reign at the Russian Imperial Ballet. Petipa was born on the threshold of the Romantic Age and had been a part of it; he danced with Elssler as early as 1841, his father, Jean Antoine Petipa, was a successful dancer and teacher (he also went to Russia as an instructor), and his brother Lucien was a dancer and choreographer of note, but Marius led the ballet out of the Romantic Age and into a new dance era. The technique of classical ballet, as we know it today, is the fruit of Petipa's genius.

Of course, we have advanced technically since Petipa's era —Fokine's artistic revolution, the influences of modern dance and ethnic forms have exerted tremendous influences—but pure, classical technique as taught in ballet schools around the world and as displayed in many of the works of George Balanchine is firmly rooted in the tradition established by Petipa. In fact, Marius Petipa is justly considered to be the Father of Classical Ballet.

It is easy to say, "Aha! Ballets which preceded him are still with us—the old, old, *La Fille Mal Gardée,* the immortal *Giselle,* and many another." But we forget that the *Giselle* we see today is Petipa's restaging of Coralli's old masterpiece and that advances in technique, unheard of in Grisi's time, are included in it. If his original creations, *The Sleeping*

Beauty among them, set new standards of technique, so also did his mounting of older ballets by his choreographic predecessors.

Ballet technique, under Petipa, advanced not only because of the demands placed upon dancers through his own creative processes but also because dancers available to him had capabilities which simply waited for exploitation. He recognized what a new generation of dancers could do, and he used his choreographic genius to afford them all manner of virtuosic challenges. From Italy to St. Petersburg came Virginia Zucchi, a fiery actress-dancer, and the now legendary Pierina Legnani, the first to execute the famous sequence of thirty-two fouettés in Act III of *Swan Lake*. Right down to the mid-twentieth century, the fouettés, as Legnani introduced them in 1895, remain the standard example of the ballerina's technical prowess. Some later dancers have accomplished double fouettés and dazzling variations on the steps known and done in Legnani's day, but the virtuosity which she, her colleagues and her immediate successors introduced during the Petipa regime is still definitive of the technique of the bravura dancer.

The Petipa regime spanned more than half a century of ballet development in Russia. In 1847, when only twenty-five, Petipa went to the Imperial Theater in St. Petersburg and contributed his services first as a dancer, then as a stager of ballets and an instructor and finally as chief choreographer until his retirement in 1903. From 1862, when he originated the triumphantly successful *The Daughter of Pharaoh*, until the end of his career, he created more than fifty full-length ballets (three and four acts long) and innumerable shorter choreographic pieces. Nearly a century later, his ballets and

his restagings of certain Romantic Age ballets are staples in
the repertories of Soviet troupes. His *The Sleeping Beauty*
has almost become a trademark of Britain's Royal Ballet, and
in whole or in part (the last act divertissement is a popular
one-acter usually called *Aurora's Wedding*), it is to be found
in companies around the world.

Swan Lake, which Petipa outlined in detail and which he
co-choreographed with his enormously gifted and too often
neglected assistant, Lev Ivanov, is quite probably to this day
the biggest box-office attraction in all ballet, with the possible exception of that holiday favorite for children, *The Nutcracker,* which Petipa commissioned from Tchaikovsky but
which Ivanov actually choreographed. The Petipa name defines the age in which he created *Bayaderka* (*La Bayadère*),
which boasts what is probably the most spectacular entrance
for a corps de ballet (in sequence, an ensemble of girls are
shown making entrances in arabesque, one by one, until the
entire stage is filled with girls in white executing the same
design) that has ever been devised. His *Don Quixote* is a
constant favorite in the Soviet Union, and the glittering
Grand Pas de Deux from it is a showpiece for the world's
greatest ballerinas and premiers danseurs.

Then there is *Raymonda,* which has found its way in its
entirety or in excerpt into the repertories of many companies.
Yes, certain Petipa ballets are forgotten or retired, but he
evolved a formula (which was his strength and his final
weakness) that consisted of a dramatic tale, projected
through pantomime and dancing, along with spectacular
solos, duets, trios and the like done in purely classical technique plus colorful "character" or national dances, the ma-

zurka, the polonaise, the echoes of Spain or China done, not with ethnologic authenticity, but with tasteful dash.

Finally, Petipa made sure that all the component arts of ballet—music, story, decor—should serve his choreography, for dance came first. So it was that he actually ordered of his composers "music by the yard." Even Tchaikovsky followed his instructions and composed scores for ballets in accordance with Petipa's measure-by-measure descriptions of what he wanted.

Under Petipa, the Russian Imperial Ballet reached a zenith which was to make Russian ballet the criterion of ballet perfection in the eyes of the world and which saw the creation of masterpieces of enduring popularity. Could ballet possibly go any further? Yes, it could. It had to. Even Petipa was not immune from rebellion. And the rebellion came with Michel Fokine, who issued, in a manifesto, a whole new concept of ballet creativity, and with it a new theater ballet age presided over by Serge Diaghileff. Petipa and his masterworks would not die—they would be dislodged temporarily while the art of dance progressed, but they would be back. The twentieth century had something to say, balletically, in its own way.

Fokine believed that every theme, locale or period demanded the creation of new movements suitable to the situation. He did not flee from the classical ballet training, as did the Americans Isadora Duncan and Ruth St. Denis, who abjured ballet technique completely and created wholly new schools of dance. But Fokine was unwilling to place bits of chinoiserie on top of classical steps and call it Chinese or to do a work, such as *Daphnis and Chloe*, evoking ancient

Greece, and put the dancers in the standard powder-puff-shaped tutus.

Fokine, influenced by the impact of Isadora Duncan (she toured Russia first in 1905) with her free movements, her dedication to (not mimicry of) the Greek ideal and her un-

Classical

Romantic

TUTUS

orthodox costuming, spurted ahead with his own reforms, reforms which he had, of course, pondered before he had ever seen Isadora.

So it was that a new manifestation of Russian ballet accomplishment exploded in Europe—in western Europe, not, at first, in St. Petersburg. The Imperial Theater was slow to accept departures from the norm. So although Fokine did create new ballets in his homeland, it was Serge Diaghileff, exporting his Ballets Russes to the West, who nurtured this restless rebel. From 1909, when the Diaghileff troupe made its Paris debut, through succeeding years, Fokine stunned the ancient citadel of ballet, Paris, with his then avant-garde creations. The wild Tartar warriors, leaping, whirling, stalking, in *Prince Igor*—why, what did they have to do with ballet? The principal female figure, Zobeide, in *Scheherazade* did not even wear toe shoes! *Petrouchka*—recreating carnival time in old Russia and combining it with a fantasy in which puppets suffer the emotional pangs of mortals. Was this ballet as Taglioni or the later Petipa knew it? No. But it was ballet.

Fokine was not out to reproduce ethnic dance forms. He was wholly creative, but he did want to capture the spirit, the color, the flavors, say, of the Tartars in his *Prince Igor*, and to this end, he wove pirouettes and air turns (executed with animal vigor rather than with elegant exactitude) into a choreographic fabric which contained images of crouching warriors, archers straining at their bows and Oriental girls moving sinuously around a campfire.

Although many of his most successful works mirrored his interest in themes derived from many races, cultures and periods, his command of classicism is forever proclaimed in his *Les Sylphides*, a tribute in abstract form to that historic, romantic ballet of an earlier era, *La Sylphide*. And what of that immortal solo, *The Dying Swan?* It is said that he created it in a matter of minutes for Anna Pavlova, but it became not only Pavlova's trademark but also a symbol of ballet beauty for decades to come. And in its modest length, it contains Fokine's principles. The movements of the feet are chiefly classical pas de bourrées, but these were selected out of the vast vocabulary of traditional ballet because they suggested gliding or floating. Upon them, he placed arms and hands which fluttered as if they were wings—this was not rigid port de bras in the classical sense, but still the contours of ballet were present—and the head moved as if it were the extension of a long and graceful neck. Here, indeed, ballet tradition and dance imaginativeness were masterfully wedded in a work which was neither a trick nor a tour de force. This was death. It was death being experienced by a beautiful creature who did not know what was happening. Does anyone really, deeply care that a long-necked bird dies? Fokine, through his *Swan*, found a universal way of communicating the sadness of death, the ironic closeness of inspiration and expiration.

Fokine, then, expanded the horizons of ballet with new movements as well as new concepts. Leonide Massine, who followed him in the Diaghileff troupe, went even further. Isadora had danced to the symphonic works of the great composers, to the accompaniment of shrill cries of protest from cautious music lovers. Massine did the same for ballet with a series of symphonic ballets, ranging from Beethoven to Shostakovitch. And Pavlova, the independent one, toured the world, and through her performing genius aroused such enthusiasm that little girls and their mothers, from Bangor, Maine, to San Diego, California, dreamed of careers in ballet. Wasn't your daughter another Pavlova? And to accommodate this dream, ballet schools sprang up everywhere. There would never be another Pavlova. But ballet had made a comeback in America, not just on the great stages but in communities large and small.

Diaghileff had extended the range of ballet not only through the choreographic artistry of the Fokines and the Massines and ultimately the Balanchines but through a concept of theater ballet which invited the collaboration of great composers (Stravinsky, among them) and great painters and librettists.

The Diaghileff Age was a fabulous age—one that saw ballet reborn in western Europe (Russia itself has yet to catch up with it), one that reestablished the prestige of ballet as an equal to opera and symphony, drama and painting. When Diaghileff died (in 1929), the ballet seemed to die with him. This man, who did not dance, choreograph, compose or paint, had presided over, directed, galvanized, created a ballet era. He was gone.

The ballet world seemed to fall apart once its master, its bully, its genius had died. But not for long. A new Ballet Russe came into being in the early 1930's, and in America, a resurgence of ballet was manifested coast to coast.

The magical year was 1933. S. Hurok, the impresario, imported the newly reconstituted Ballet Russe de Monte Carlo to America. He lost close to $100,000 on the venture—two decades later, he would gross $4,000,000 on his dance attractions alone—but it was the beginning of ballet's climb to new and unexpected heights of popularity in America.

In that same year, the Atlanta Civic Ballet, with roots going back to 1929, the oldest "regional" ballet company in the United States, was born, and out in San Francisco, Adolph Bolm, the great Diaghileff dancer-mime, laid the groundwork, through the opera, for the establishing of the San Francisco Ballet, a regional ballet destined, in another quarter of a century, to win international renown.

And, in 1934, the American Ballet, headed by George Balanchine (who had come to America the preceding year, at the invitation of Lincoln Kirstein and Edward M. M. Warburg, to form the School of American Ballet), gave its first performances. Through a series of metamorphoses, this company would eventually emerge, under Balanchine-Kirstein direction, as the New York City Ballet, one of the most celebrated ballet troupes in the world, known to most dance followers as "the Balanchine company."

The Ballet Russe de Monte Carlo, which eventually became an American company, brought with it all manner of marvels and novelties. It introduced to America Alexandra Danilova (she had escaped from the Soviet Union in company with Balanchine and Tamara Geva and had joined the Diaghileff Ballets Russes), one of the great ballerinas of our century; the three highly publicized "Baby Ballerinas," Irina Baronova, Tamara Toumanova and Tatiana Riabouchinska; major male dancers, among them Massine himself (who had danced and choreographed at New York's Roxy Theater in the late 1920's) and, subsequently, the young Frederic Franklin.

It also introduced to the American public during the decade which followed its United States debut Massine's symphonic ballets and those two perennial favorites which he also created, *Le Beau Danube* and *Gaité Parisienne*. The prolifiic Massine dominated the repertory of the Ballet Russe de Monte Carlo for many seasons, but that repertory did not neglect the important works of Fokine, both old and new, and such classics as *Swan Lake* (in one-act version) and *Aurora's Wedding* and various pas de deux from the Petipa era, *Giselle* and other pieces.

The Ballet Russe de Monte Carlo, glamorous and glittering, was by all odds the chief ballet attraction in America in the 1930's, but it did not go unrivaled. The American Ballet and its relations, the Ballet Caravan, the American Ballet Caravan (and, eventually, Ballet Society and the New York City Ballet) made their marks. Balanchine's first creations for the American company, among them his immortal *Serenade*, invited the attention of the art world to this choreographic genius.

The American Ballet itself was even engaged as resident ballet company for the Metropolitan Opera (1935–1938), but Balanchine was too avant-garde for the Met and his departures from operatic traditions caused dissatisfaction, friction and controversy in opera circles. The association ended amid a good deal of bitterness and publicity.

In 1940, another major contender for dominance of ballet in America was born, the Ballet Theatre (later named the American Ballet Theatre). As suggested by its name, the concept of the new company was to give equal accent to theater, and to this end, under the initial guidance of Richard Pleasant, it established three wings of enterprise: one was designed to revive and renew the classics (Anton Dolin headed this department); another was to form an English ballet area dominated by the dramatic ballets of Antony Tudor; and there was the Americana wing, involving the talents of Eugene Loring and Agnes de Mille.

The company's premiere was enormously exciting, but although the repertory grew steadily, increasing its scope to the point that it was regarded as the broadest and probably the finest ballet repertory in the world, it faced continuing hardships. Bookings were difficult, for Americans had assoc-

ciated the word "Russian" with the word "ballet" and nothing could budge them. They were just not interested in an
American product. On one tour, for example, S. Hurok, who
booked the company briefly, had the posters outside theaters
show "Ballet Theatre" in very small letters and then in huge
ones, "THE GREATEST IN RUSSIAN BALLET." That was
how to sell American Ballet.

So it was that the cornerstones of a solid twentieth-century
American ballet establishment were the Ballet Russe de
Monte Carlo, the American Ballet (and its related groups),
the Ballet Theatre and the various regional ballets.

England's Alicia Markova and Dolin, the most famous
team in ballet, became almost household words through their
long association with Ballet Theatre and through appearances on the Broadway stage. Danilova was potent box office,
and many other European dance stars became familiar to
dance-minded audiences. But, in this ballet renascence, the
Americans were playing a major part. In Ballet Theatre alone
we witnessed the emerging of Nora Kaye, Jerome Robbins,
Rosella Hightower, John Kriza, the Cuban-born but American trained Alicia Alonso and many others. Up and up they
moved to become ballerinas, premiers danseurs, choreographers.

Before long, Tallchief would become a major name in ballet as two sisters of American Indian origin, Maria and Marjorie, brought new and electrifying presences to the whole
world of ballet. Indeed, one of them, Maria, during one year
became the highest paid ballerina in the world.

Choreographically, America took the ballet lead in the
1940's, 1950's and into the 1960's. Robbins, starting with his
Fancy Free for Ballet Theatre in 1944, soon became one of

the most sought after choreographers in the world, not only for the ballet itself but also for Broadway musicals, movies, television. Balanchine's greatest output—and he is the most prolific of choreographers—had taken place during his three-decades-plus in America, working with American dancers.

Agnes de Mille launched her fusion of American folk dance (and folk forms of other countries) with ballet and paralleled Robbins' successes in ballet, musicals, TV.

Robbins' use of jazz elements, De Mille's folk inclusions, the strong influences of modern dance, an extended use of dramatic gesture (freely devised as distinct from traditional mime), all contributed to the swiftly expanding vocabulary of ballet in America. The classical base remained in the classroom and was, of course, used on stage in classical ballets, both old and newly created, but the American dancer had to be a master of more than this one technique. He had to be adept at jazz, at modern dance, in folk or ethnic measures, for even a corps de ballet girl or boy might be expected, on a given program, to dance in *Swan Lake,* the modern, dramatic *Fall River Legend,* the folk *Wind in the Mountains* and a completely modern dance work such as *Sargasso.*

But this remarkable ballet renascence and flourishing was not limited to America alone, although Americans were way ahead in the vanguard of creativity. In London, in 1926, an ex-Diaghileff dancer was engaged to stage the opera-ballets at the Old Vic Theater. Her name was Ninette de Valois (Edris Stannus). This ambitious, talented and indomitable woman soon extended her balletic toehold and found herself planted on a new British ballet. Under her direction, the Vic-Wells Ballet came into being; the necessary ballet school was established at Sadler's Wells.

In due course, the Vic-Wells Ballet became the Sadler's Wells Ballet and under that title outgrew its insular beginnings, for in its tours to the continent of Europe and to America, it stirred audiences to wild pitches of enthusiasm. In fact, in America, the public receded from its long-held position that ballet, to be good, had to be Russian. Suddenly, it had to be British. Equally suddenly a new name, Margot Fonteyn, became synonymous with the term "prima ballerina."

The company's first great star was Markova, who had been a teen-age prodigy in the Diaghileff company, and it was Markova who aided the Sadler's Wells Ballet's swift rise to success through the glory of her own dancing, not only in the great classics but also in a variety of modern ballets created by a rising band of young English choreographers, among them Frederick Ashton.

When Markova left to win new fame in America, the doleful cried out that the Sadler's Wells company was doomed. To the contrary, the coming of World War II saw the Sadler's Wells Ballet attain unprecedented heights of popularity as a war-torn nation found momentary escape and beauty in the magic of *The Sleeping Beauty* and in the personal magic of Markova's successor, Fonteyn.

The rise of the Sadler's Wells Ballet to international repute with respect to both performing brilliance and choreographic invention warranted governmental recognition; thus, by Royal Charter from Queen Elizabeth II, the Sadler's Wells Ballet became the Royal Ballet.

There were other stirrings. In Copenhagen, the Royal Danish Ballet, without discarding its great and unique Bournonville heritage, sought to extend its horizons. Fokine came to Denmark to stage several of his masterpieces for the versatile

Danes. Later, the repertory was broadened to include works by Balanchine, by Ashton, by contemporary Danish choreographers. And Vera Volkova, one of the great teachers of the century, came to Denmark to balance, through her teaching, the Bournonville technique with the glittering style evolved by Petipa's Russia.

In France, the Paris Opera Ballet stirred, trying to break out of the lethargy which had transformed the one–time capital of ballet into an extravagantly costumed bore. But young rebels, such as Roland Petit, gave French ballet a new spurt by breaking away from the opera and soaring forth on adventurous wings.

Italy, which had given birth to ballet, or at least to the ancestor of ballet, remained creatively quiescent into the sixth decade of this century. But the Swedish ballet spurted ahead, adding modern dance works as well as new stagings of classics to its repertory, and this very Western art form began to take hold in Turkey and in Japan. Indeed, its ancient heritage echoed around the world from Canada to New Zealand, from West to East.

Lafontaine, in the Paris of 1681, had glided gracefully across a stage, wearing her opulent and cumbersome costumes with grace and moving with charming deportment. Nearly three hundred years later, her artistic descendants were wearing classical tutus, which were little more than exaggerated powder puffs encircling the hips, and wearing blocked-toe shoes, which enabled them to accomplish vertiginous spins, incredible balances, tattoo-like hops on the perilous tips of their pointes.

The Italians of the nineteenth century had introduced fire, virtuosic and dramatic, into ballet. The Danes had imbued ballet with a special exuberance. The Russians established an enduring classicism, a model for the world to follow; the English counteracted the Bolshoi Ballet's flamboyant acrobatics with an aristocratic lyricism, and America gave its expansiveness, its athleticism and its rebellious unconcern for tradition-at-any-cost to international ballet.

What had ballet turned into? Its connection with Catherine de Medici, with Louis XIV, with Lafontaine was mainly ancestral; still it was ballet. In the process of its evolution, it not only had added new steps, new prowess and new styles to its vocabulary of action but had also become truly international as its movements and patterns and rhythms were colored by the cultures, the peoples, the personalities who adopted it.

An American *Les Sylphides* is very different from a British *Les Sylphides*, although every step, every gesture, every pattern, every progression, is exactly the same. The difference is a matter of accent. The President of the United States and the Queen of England speak the same tongue, but do they sound alike? Both are comprehensible, but one is unmistakably English and the other undeniably American. Accents in movement are equally idiomatic.

Ballet, by the latter half of the twentieth century, reached a new peak of achievement, a new apex of esthetic accomplishment and popular approval, because it was nurtured not by one man or one nation but by the world itself. As in musical form, its variations upon a theme, ballet, were limitless.

"Ballet" is also a company.

It can be of almost any size, say, from ten dancers to over two hundred. It can be supported by the state, such as the

Royal Ballets of Denmark or Sweden are, or as the Soviet and the Paris Opera Ballets are. Or it can exist, as it does in America, through the financial assistance by individuals or by grants from foundations. A ballet company on a large scale cannot pay its own way, no matter how large the attendance at its performances. Operating costs are high and production expenses are astronomical.

In a ballet troupe, rank is almost as strict as it is in the army. Of course, a small company, composed of ten or twelve dancers, may be so constituted that it has no stars and no strictly corps de ballet dancers but, rather, soloists of equal rank who may double, from one ballet production to another, between corps and solo work.

Strictly, and traditionally, the performers, the dancers, in a classical ballet troupe include, on the lowest level, the corps de ballet, next the coryphées, soloists, ballerina and danseur, prima ballerina and premier danseur (or, in France, première danseuse and premier danseur étoiles).

The dancers of the corps de ballet (literally, "the body of the ballet") are ensemble dancers. They move together as a unit in patterns, consisting of poses and steps, planned for them by a choreographer. They do not necessarily move as a block in mass formations (although they can and do), for some designs, such as the leaping exits of the Wilis in *Giselle*, might be described as sequential actions, that is, a sort of follow-the-leader routine.

Coryphées are those dancers who rank between the corps de ballet and the soloists. These would be those selected to perform in small groups, perhaps a pas de six (dance for six). The term "coryphée" (or, in the masculine, "coryphé") was in standard use in the Russian Imperial Ballet, but it has been only rarely used in America. A somewhat equivalent designation is "semi-soloist," (or "demi-soloist") a rather insulting-sounding title but actually a trifle higher than coryphée, for the semi-soloist may actually have a distinctive step to do in conjunction with the designs being performed by the corps.

Soloists are exactly what you would expect—they dance alone on stage, or in pairs or trios. A soloist, male or female, may have a solo number, usually called a variation, to perform by himself. The stage can be empty of performers except for him, or the corps may be posed in back or placed about the stage as the choreographer determines. In *Giselle*, for example, in the frequently interpolated Peasant Pas de Deux, the peasants (the corps de ballet and coryphées) watch, and even the ballet's leading characters (including the ballerina) look on as the two soloists dance their duet (pas de deux).

Soloists, because they must be accomplished technicians and experienced artists in order to do their solo assignments effectively, occasionally are given opportunities to dance leading roles. This, however, does not give them the right to assume the titles of ballerina or premier danseur, for this is a trial, a testing and, if they are successful, they may eventually be promoted to ballerina or danseur rank.

This brings us to the word "ballerina." It is a very special word which designates a very special, and quite rare, status. And it is sorely misused. Non-dance writers for newspapers or magazines—columnists or general reporters—use the word "ballerina" as if it meant simply a female ballet dancer, and they use it to refer to a girl in the corps de ballet or even a student who manages to stagger up onto pointe. Well, this is like calling a private in the army a colonel or a general.

Occasionally you may see a poster which advertises fifty ballerinas in one production. There are barely more than fifty ballerinas in the entire world; there is only one prima ballerina to a company, and there has not been an officially appointed prima ballerina assoluta (the "absolute") since the last Czar of Russia conferred that rank on Mathilde Kschessinska of the Russian Imperial Ballet at the Maryinsky Theater (now the Kirov) in St. Petersburg. Since that time, Alexandra Danilova in her mature years and Dame Margot Fonteyn have been referred to as primas ballerinas assolutas, and with justification, because of the worldwide esteem in which they have been held and because of the acknowledged unique artistry of each.

Probably the closest definition that we can find for "ballerina" is "star." She is not simply any old toe dancer, any pretty girl who works in a ballet company. She is truly a star with top billing to match her artistry and, of course, her impact as a personality and her drawing power at the box office. If she is the prima ballerina, she is the undisputed performing apex of that organization structured like a pyramid with its wide base in the corps de ballet.

A female dancer, then, becomes a ballerina when her dancing skills of an unusually high order are recognized by the director of a company and by the public who have taken note of her ever growing accomplishments. Usually, she must prove her worth in those standard classics in which she is put on trial and in which she can be compared with her illustrious predecessors or her contemporaries of ballerina rank.

It is, of course, in today's ballet very possible for the aspirant to the title of ballerina to win her way by superb interpretations of contemporary ballets, dramatic (which call for an actress-dancer) or abstract (which demand purity of line in movement as well as technical brilliance), but few ballerinas are truly content until they have attempted the challenging principal roles in *Swan Lake* or, perhaps, *Giselle*.

But as essential as the ballerina may be to the stature of a great company, she is, surprisingly enough, outranked. The director of a ballet company is her superior (and she must also heed the instructions of the ballet master, the régisseur, the choreographers and her teachers—yes, she goes to class daily, and although she is treated with proper deference, she is subject, and willingly, to the instruction supplied by the teacher of the ballet lesson).

The direction of a company may take several forms. A familiar one is that in which there is a general director and an artistic director; or there may be, simply, either a director or an artistic director; sometimes there are co-directors; and, occasionally, the ballet master is also the director. Whatever the title, the function of the director is to run the company: he formulates policy, he determines the size of the company, he selects repertory, he decides what new ballets should be commissioned and which old works should be revived, refurbished or totally restaged. On the basis of his budget, he strives constantly to develop his company to the point that it can rival or, he hopes, surpass all other ballet groups which fall into a given category (small or large, contemporary or classical, etc.).

A major function of the ballet master (or mistress) is to keep the members of a ballet company at the highest level of technical accomplishment. In royal and state theaters, company members attend daily class in their home theater, as they have since childhood, where they are taught and coached by the resident faculty. In America, where there is no state ballet institution, the dancers may go to any teacher of their choice, although a good many study at whatever school is associated with their company. (The School of American Ballet is the official school of the New York City Ballet, just as the Ballet Theatre School is allied with the American Ballet Theatre.)

When a ballet company is touring, its dancers cannot, of course, attend regular classes at various hours at their customary studios. The rigors of a tour, of constant performing, demand that the dancers remain in tip-top condition. Here, the ballet master or his assistant assumes the daily responsibility of adhering to a training program. A company class is given each day, usually on the stage of the theater where the troupe is to perform. If travel time permits, there may be a full-length lesson during the day and a warm-up class before performance time.

If the company visits major cities, its dancers may elect to take a lesson from some local teacher of renown, but the company class is always available, whether the ballet has arrived in a big town with many ballet studios or on a university campus where there are no ballet instructors.

When the tour is a matter of one-night stands, the ballet master's daily classes keep the dancers, no matter how tired they may be, at performing pitch, and postpone, if not entirely avoid, that weary, disinterested, somewhat tacky look that a company may have as it nears the end of an arduous tour.

Rehearsals of a ballet may be under the supervision of the choreographer himself when he is available, or of the ballet master or of a répétiteur, whose duty it is to see that ballets are properly rehearsed and that the choreographer's designs and intents are in no way violated. Occasionally, a company will employ the services of a régisseur, one who is something more than a stage manager, for it is he who is responsible for obtaining the total stage picture desired by all of the collaborators involved in a ballet production. Sometimes, because of years of experience, he may actually conduct rehearsals on stage; this is particularly true if a given work is a traditional ballet from the past or one for which a living choreographer cannot be present for final polishing before a performance.

The staff of a ballet company consists of many other experts. These include the stage manager and his assistants, a company manager (a popular figure on tour since it is he who acts as paymaster), the wardrobe mistress and her assistants, the electrician. Indeed, when a big company is performing, a big stage crew is essential. A ballet troupe may also have a designer of lighting as a permanent staff member, although many choreographers prefer to have lighting designers of their own choice plan the lighting effects for their own ballets (just as they customarily select the designers of scenery or decor and costumes).

And there are still other major jobs to be filled, among them the tremendously important post of director of publicity. His task and that of his associates are to see that the company he works for becomes known, that its accomplishments are reported over as wide an area as possible. He informs newspapers, periodicals of all kinds, radio and television programs, theater groups, schools, student bodies and the like of the activities of the company he represents: dates of seasons in a given theater or touring schedules; repertory listings and special publicity on new creations, new members of the company, guest artists and interesting collaborations; advance promotion on a city-by-city basis in which posters are prominently displayed, advertisements placed in local publications, interviews arranged for and a myriad of other duties, all aimed to promote interest in the company.

The staff of a ballet company varies from group to group, as I have indicated. You may run across the title of executive director or administrative director or something of the sort. The designations may indeed vary but there are key functions which must be performed in every ballet troupe no matter how the staff is organized with respect to titles.

A ballet company necessarily employs the services of artists other than the dancers themselves. All-important artistic collaboration comes from choreographers, composers, musical arrangers, orchestra conductors, pit musicians, designers of costumes, designers of settings, designers of lighting effects, librettists (when story-ballets are involved) or poets and playwrights when a ballet combines movement with dialogue or narration. There are occasions when singers and actors are artistic participants in a ballet performance.

How these various collaborators and the arts in which they are expert are pooled to make a single work of dance art is a subject in itself, and this brings us to our third definition of the word "ballet"—a theatrical production.

A ballet is a stage creation. Beaujoyeulx, the choreographer of *Le Ballet Comique de la Reine* in 1581, defined a ballet as "a geometrical arrangement of numerous people dancing together under a diverse harmony of many instruments." But no single definition of a ballet is wholly satisfactory. Ballet, as a stage creation, is a production conceived and executed in ballet style; such a ballet is usually composed of four major elements: movement (dance or gesture or mime), music (traditional ballet scores, music originally composed for other than dance use, specially commissioned music, sound effects), design (costumes and scenery or decor—often lighting designs are used in lieu of scenery) and theme (dramatic, comic, abstract, etc.).

The range of ballet has grown to such an extent over the centuries that there are many categories of ballet, sufficient, in fact, to account for almost every taste.

Some persons prefer the so-called white ballets. These are the old-time classics such as *Swan Lake* or the much later *Les Sylphides;* they are called "white" chiefly because the girls of the corps de ballet wear white tutus or entirely white costumes or, perhaps, a pastel color which sets them off in lovely mass designs against the background or the setting. Strictly speaking, such ballets are not exclusively white by any means. But "white" has come to mean a fairytale ballet in all likelihood set to music of Tchaikovsky danced in classical style and in classical dress, either the tutus of the length popular in the Romantic Age of ballet or the short tutus of the dazzling Petipa era of the Russian Imperial Ballet.

In the other corner, we find those ballet followers who seem to be allergic to enchanted swans, sleeping princesses and assortments of wilis, pixies and dryads. These look for modern ballets which have adult themes and emotional conflicts which disturb the onlooker and not simply amuse or exhilarate him. They may also enjoy avant-garde ballets or abstractions set to electronic scores, just as the lovers of "white" ballets usually extend their tastes to include contemporary ballets—such as those Balanchine has created to symphonic scores—which retain classical steps and style.

Giselle and *La Sylphide* are the superb examples of the ballet art of the Romantic Age. They are both "white" ballets, they both relate reality to the supernatural, they are both romantic tragedies in which the heroines are desirable but unattainable, they both rely upon mime to forward the plot, they both balance elements of purely classical dancing with balleticized folk dance measures, and they are both vehicles for the ballerina and her special art.

Ballets such as these demand elaborate staging, for they are only partly dancing—they are illustrated stories. *La Sylphide* requires wires so that the dead Sylphide, at the close of the ballet, may float heavenwards, borne by attendant sylphs. Even the witches in a sort of macabre prologue to Act II are invited to fly about on their broomsticks. At one time, wires for flying Wilis were used in *Giselle*.

So it is that there is no place for cutting corners, with respect to production, in *La Sylphide, Giselle* or any other Romantic Age ballet or in a contemporary re-creation of such a period piece (for example, Frederick Ashton's *Ondine*). In the first acts of *La Sylphide* and *Giselle* there must be plenty of peasant characters roaming about, and in the second acts, full complements of sylphides and wilis must be present to populate the woodland glades.

Not every ballet of the Romantic Age ended in tragedy. Indeed, most had happy endings, but the tragedies survived the age itself. Of the comedies, only the earlier *The Whims of Cupid and the Ballet Master* and *La Fille Mal Gardée* and the later *Coppélia* have come down to us today.

Of the existing ballets of the Romantic Age, none has remained completely unchanged with the passage of years; certainly, the principal alterations have to do with the development of the toe shoe. The great ballerinas of the Romantic Age were limited in their toe technique, while today's ballerinas have achieved a new and glittering level of virtuosity on pointe. Audiences, accustomed to this in ballet today, would hardly settle for barely more than three or four simple steps on pointe. So today's ballerinas now execute various pointe displays which have been incorporated into the old ballets over the years. It is likely that in a ballet such as *La Sylphide*, which, in its Danish version, has been danced almost continuously, the choreographic outlines for ensemble work and for solo variations remain the same, but where half-toe, or demi-pointe, was once used, now the full pointe, where appropriate, is utilized.

The ballerina and her colleagues cannot, however, tamper with the performing style of Romantic ballet. And that style is best described by the word "romantic" itself. Elusiveness, tenderness, delicacy and softness of line are among its characteristics. Virtuosity and glamour may be present, but they are of a different sort from the bravura and the glitter of the Age of Petipa.

Perhaps a good way to pinpoint what we mean by romantic style is to quote Nora Kaye, the greatest dramatic ballerina of the mid-twentieth century. Miss Kaye catapulted to fame in contemporary dramatic ballets by Antony Tudor, Jerome Robbins and others; in most, there were psychological processes clearly expressed choreographically. But when Miss

Kaye first essayed *Giselle*, she had problems and, oddly enough, most of them had to do with the intensely dramatic Mad Scene which brings Act I to a close. Miss Kaye described the flaws in her interpretation by saying, "I was too damn clinical. I showed the audience what a madwoman was like. For 'Giselle,' that is wrong. It is romantic, and you should go mad prettily, with grace and a delicate air."

And that just about describes the key to the ballet of the Romantic Age.

I have said that there are no shortcuts, no bargains to be had in mounting ballets of the Romantic Age. The same is true of the ballets of the Age of Petipa, for with Petipa and the Russian Imperial Ballet, ballet itself reached a new degree of splendor not only in dance techniques but in the staging of the works themselves. Sleeping Beauties live in soaring castles, not against unadorned black drapes, and enchanted swan maidens face their lot by a lake and not on bare stages. The illusion of which the theater is capable is an essential for those ballets which are truly theatrical spectacles.

The ballets of Petipa and Ivanov are, in a sense, an extension of the Romantic Age, for Petipa himself was a product of that era. Inspired by the fiery talents as dancer and actress of the Italian Virginia Zucchi, the dazzling virtuosity of Italy's Pierina Legnani and the swiftly advancing technique of ballet itself, Petipa and Ivanov, together and separately, created ballets which would glorify the ballerina. If Odette, the gentle Queen of the Swans in *Swan Lake*, was an evocation of the softness, sadness and shyness of many heroines of the Romantic Age, the evil Odile in *Swan Lake* represented the new powers, the hauteur, the regal grandeur of the ballerina of a later age. That both roles were danced by one ballerina was indicative of the progress made in ballet and the increased challenges facing the ballerina.

The pointe became all-important as the focal point of the ballerina's virtuosity. More and more feats of skill were accomplished on pointe as the shoe developed from the simple, soft affair (strengthened by a bit of darning) it had been to a shoe blocked with protective materials, glue, harder soles and even nails.

The increased use of pointe introduced a new sharpness of attack upon a movement into the ballerina's art. As she became, during the long reign of Petipa, an increasingly glittering figure, imperious in manner, a conqueror of the physical hazards attendant upon dancing on that tiny and perilous pointe, the style necessarily changed too. Tchaikovsky's ballet scores, once thought to be "too symphonic," also affected the form of choreography and the style of performing.

The Petipa formula for a full-length ballet, usually in three or four acts and with several scenes, included mime episodes through which the story was told, dances for the corps de ballet, pas de deux for the hero and heroine, solos, trios and other groupings all in classical style or in demi-caractère, plus peasant dances, character dances (a court jester, for example) and national dances (czardas, jota, polonaise, etc.).

These ballets were also so constructed that excerpts—usually a bravura pas de deux—were danceable outside the context of the ballet itself, just as an aria may be taken from an opera and sung in concert. Thus, we have such showpieces as the so-called Black Swan Pas de Deux from *Swan Lake*, the Grand Pas de Deux from *Don Quixote* and *The Nutcracker* Pas de Deux, which are invariably, when danced by great technicians, genuine highlights on a divertissement program, often receiving more applause and bravos than, say, a complete one-act ballet. They are also both serviceable and popular vehicles for the ballerina and the premier danseur when they appear as concert performers with a symphony orchestra.

So if *La Sylphide* and *Giselle* are prime examples of the Romantic Age, it may be said that *The Sleeping Beauty, The Nutcracker* and *Swan Lake* are the epitome of the Age of Petipa.

Classical ballet, however, does not belong to a single age. It is reborn, renewed and redirected for every era. The heir to Petipa was not Michel Fokine, although chronologically Fokine came at the appointed time. Fokine, although he was trained in and was a master of the classics, was chiefly concerned with extending ballet from its classical base into new areas of dance; *Petrouchka* is a good example of this.

The true heir to Petipa was a man much younger than Fokine but one also reared with the Russian Imperial Ballet (and later the Soviet State Ballet) at the Maryinsky. He was, of course, George Balanchine.

Balanchine—very probably the most celebrated single name in all ballet of the mid-twentieth century—is not an imitator of Petipa but, as I have said, an heir. The classical step and the classical gesture of Petipa are present in Balanchine's choreographies and so also are the old master's concern for brilliant exploitation of the ballerina's skills and for the creating of superlative pure dance designs for corps de ballet, ensembles and small units. The phrase "pure dance" is a key to Balanchine's classicism. Not only has Balanchine extended the movement vocabulary of the Petipa Age into new and undreamed-of virtuosities and combinations, but he has also, in the majority of his most successful ballets, cut away the dramatic elements of Petipa's day and created "pure dance" ballets, that is, ballets with no story, no plot, no characters other than the dancers themselves. This sort of ballet, then, has often been referred to as "abstract."

Examples of this might be *Theme and Variations*, to music of Tchaikovsky, which he choreographed for the American Ballet Theatre, and his *Raymonda Variations*, danced by his own New York City Ballet and, in related forms, by other companies. Neither has a plot, both are pure classical dance, both have their choreographic forms rooted in the music. These are ballets best described as dance for the sake of dancing.

Balanchine, of course, makes many other types of ballet: dramatic ballets (*The Prodigal Son*), romantic ballets (*La Sonnambula* or *The Night Shadow*), full-length narrative ballets filled with mime (*Don Quixote*), avant-garde ballets (*Episodes*) and almost any category of ballet you care to name. But his choreographic genius seems to give especial illumination to those "pure" works which enrich the heritage of Petipa and place it in the heart of this century. Until the balletomane has seen Balanchine's *Serenade* (Tchaikovsky), with an aura of romance, a hint of sorrow brushing its purely dancing measures, he has not experienced one of the most perfect dance creations of our age, a work which ranges from the most basic of classical ballet positions for feet, arms and head to movements of electrifying force and beauty.

Balanchine, however, is not the only twentieth-century classicist. There are others, the greatest of whom—and he is Balanchine's peer—is England's Sir Frederick Ashton. His pas de deux and his ensemble dances in the classical idiom are to be found not so much in his abstract ballets (although he has been successful in this genre) as in story ballets, such as *Ondine, The Dream* or his staging of *Romeo and Juliet.* He is a master choreographer in demi-caractère, in comedy, in drama, in fantasy (he created *Illuminations* for the New York City Ballet) and particularly in romance, but his classical designs—some of the loveliest were created for Dame Margot Fonteyn—are of ineffable beauty.

The technique of classical ballet itself has long fascinated the public, and there are enormously successful ballets which are based entirely on a disclosure of the ingredients contained in the technique of ballet itself. Such ballets actually take the viewer into a theatricalized classroom where he can observe the training of the dancer.

The Royal Danish Ballet boasts two such ballets. The oldest is *Konservatoriet (The Conservatory)*, a ballet created by Bournonville in 1849 as a sort of movement recollection of the classes, conducted by the great Auguste Vestris, in Paris which Bournonville had attended. *Konservatoriet* originally had an accompanying plot; today, the story part is omitted and we see only the lesson, starting with the children and what they can do, and growing in complexity and technical challenges as the ballet reaches its conclusion. It is not only a charming ballet but also an important one historically, for it shows the technical range and the style of ballet as it was known in the world capital of ballet, Paris, in the 1820's, the dawn of the Romantic Age.

In striking contrast, yet with an intensely effective sense of sequence, is a second Danish ballet based upon the classroom. This is Harald Lander's *Etudes*, a scintillating tour de force (only a first-rate company can dare attempt it) which begins with a simple plié (the most fundamental step in ballet) through the exercises at barre (with limberings, stretches, kicks, brushes and all the fundamentals) to the most difficult of balances, turns, runs, leaps, beats and all manner of combinations thereof. *Etudes,* as danced by the Royal Danish Ballet itself, by the American Ballet Theatre and by other major companies, represents the ballet advances in technique accomplished over more than a century.

The Russians, in the 1960's, noting the international success and appeal of *Etudes,* created their own ballet on the classroom technique theme, *Ballet School,* choreographed by Asaf Messerer for the Bolshoi Ballet. It too was a smash with audiences wherever it was played. Incidentally, so fascinating to the public is such a ballet that subsequent to the producing of the Bolshoi work, Igor Moiseyev, in 1964 did a similar ballet for the Moiseyev Dance Company from Moscow (which isn't a ballet company at all but rather a highly theatricalized and technically brilliant folk dance troupe). Here, the dancers began with elementary ballet but soon, in their "staged classroom," moved on to the varieties of steps and styles demanded of them by their ethnically varied repertory.

Folk ingredients or flavors have long been important to classical ballet troupes. The Romantic Age used them liberally—*La Sylphide* had its greatly adapted Scottish dances, Fanny Elssler was famed for her *Cachucha* (Spanish), and there were many other dances which gave an ethnic nod in the general direction of Italy (Bournonville's *Napoli* is a lasting example of this), Lithuania, Poland or even gypsy encampments.

Bournonville's *Far From Denmark* is basically an elaborate tour which is used as an excuse to present an array of balleticized folk dances, including nose-rubbing Eskimos!

In the twentieth century, America has pioneered in the development of ballets which incorporate American folk dance idioms and folk customs and characteristics with ballet. Agnes de Mille's *Rodeo* and her *Wind in the Mountains* and Eugene Loring's *Billy the Kid* belong in this category of ballet. Pirouettes, double air turns—in *Billy*, for example— are superbly and excitingly adapted to the needs of a lawless braggart of the old West.

De Mille uses less ballet technique in her historic *Rodeo* (first produced in 1942 and the forerunner to that history-making musical *Oklahoma!*, which De Mille choreographed) than she does in her dramatic *Fall River Legend*, based on an American story in an American setting. In one scene, at a New England church social, the choreographer heightens social dance steps with adapted ballet actions, and for her heroine, she fuses acting with ballet steps.

Jerome Robbins's first ballet, *Fancy Free*, also combines acting and ballet, folk (this time, jazz influences) and ballet. And there are other theater pieces, produced by ballet companies which project an American heritage, not through folk dance measures or rural flavors alone, but in conjunction with the disciplines and virtuosities of international ballet technique.

Modern dance, with its accent on the total expressivity of the body and on the total freedom of the choreographer to invent (or select) the movement which best expresses a given idea, instant of drama or the like, has long since lent its powers to ballet.

There was a time, in the 1930's, when the ballet-minded and the moderns were violently opposed, when they said harsh things about each other, when they swore that any attempt at fusing the two forms, even in a passing movement phrase, was idiotic if not downright impossible. Were they not two antithetical approaches to dance? And did not modern dance come into being to counteract the shortcomings of the deeply-rooted-in-tradition ballet?

What was overlooked was that *dance* itself encompasses all manifestations and styles of rhythmic, ordered action, including ballet, and that as the horizons of choreography were extended by questing, imaginative choreographers, it was necessary to extend dance techniques and their uses to match the need.

Antony Tudor, in the majority of his most famous ballets, has interwoven modern dance, or free-style action, with ballet. He has gone even a step further in actually applying the concepts of modern dance to ballet steps. For instance, in classical ballet, the ballerina rises onto pointe in order to dance—she may do it slowly or quickly, softly or sharply or

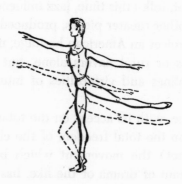

Relevé en 1st Arabesque

in any of a number of variations of the relevé. But there is a brilliant instant in Tudor's *Lilac Garden* in which he uses the very act of rising onto pointe as a climactic expression of ecstasy. It comes at that moment when the ballet's heroine, about to marry a man she does not love, awaits the final, secret farewells with her lover in the not-very-private surroundings of a garden party. She stands, tense and alert. A hand touches her shoulder. It can be only one hand. It is the only hand in the world. At its touch, she rises onto a new emotional plane, perhaps into momentary heaven. The toe shoes do not actually get her there but they mirror, in their rising, the hidden journey of her heart.

In *Pillar of Fire*, when the heroine has given her body, in defiance of family and convention, to a libertine, she contracts her body at the waist in a spasm of shame. This is pure modern dance, but linked with it in the same episodes are swift arabesque turns on pointe which, as Tudor has molded them, express the character's desperate search for escape from a world and a situation which is just too much to bear.

Tudor's *Dark Elegies*, which was first produced as far back as 1937 (and in conservative England), is much more of a theatricalized ritual of community and individual response to death than it is a formal ballet. His *Judgment of Paris* is certainly a ballet, since it is danced by ballet dancers in several ballet repertories, yet it does not have one ballet step in it! His *Dim Lustre*, on the other hand, is quite balletic, although it does contain those dramatic gestures which constitute a Tudor trademark.

De Mille's sprightly and funny *Three Virgins and a Devil* comes closer to modern dance than it does to ballet. The devil has quite a few ballet steps to execute, but the virgins have none at all. Their roles are conceived in terms of dance act-ing.

Gerald Arpino's *Incubus,* in the repertory of the Robert Joffrey Ballet, is very unballetic in the classical sense, for it finds its dramatic powers in distorted, macabre episodes composed of highly inventive dance movement and gesture.

Robbins's *The Age of Anxiety* and his *The Cage* contain much which is closely related to modern dance. Robbins himself says that he does not borrow from modern dance per se but that he creates whatever movements his themes dic-tate and that they are wholly original with him. They are. But the accomplishments of modern dance and its continu-ing exposure to public and artists alike are certain to have introduced a new dance climate which has affected, some-times directly and again indirectly, the procedures of choreo-grahphers in all areas of theater dance, from music hall to ballet.

Robbins's monumental *Les Noces,* which he created for the American Ballet Theatre's twenty-fifth anniversary sea-son in 1965, is a triumphant example of what has been slowly happening to ballet in the mid-twentieth century—that is, in-stead of the art of dance incorporating ballet within its vast, immeasurable reaches, ballet is endeavoring to incorporate all forms of theater dance within its own creative area.

The trend continues. Norman Walker, trained as a modern dancer, a choreographer of modern dance and head of a modern dance company—and successful in all three depart-ments—has been able to share his talents with the world of ballet. For the Joffrey troupe and the Harkness Ballet he choreographed real ballets, much of them in an overall ballet style, including the use of pointes. But for the Boston Ballet, he staged one of his own modern dance works and coached the ballet-trained dancers to move in modern dance ways.

The greatest name in American modern dance, Martha Graham, and the most famous name in contemporary ballet, George Balanchine, were linked in 1959 in the New York City Ballet's experimental production of *Episodes,* set to the orchestral works of the avant-garde Anton Webern. Graham, oddly enough, choreographed in more traditional theater style for her episode than did Balanchine for his, for Graham made a dance-drama, enormously effective, of the confrontation of Elizabeth I and Mary, Queen of Scots. Graham used New York City Ballet dancers as well as members of her own company in this production. Balanchine, in his section, came up with an amazing array of movement departures from ballet. One episode in the Balanchine division was actually danced by a noted modern dancer, Paul Taylor.

But *Episodes* was not alone in its transcending of presumed dance barriers in the act of performing as well as in the art of choreography. Glen Tetley, reared as a modern dancer by Hanya Holm and Martha Graham, not only turned into a star performer in the modern dance field but also made the switch to ballet when the opportunities interested him, dancing certain roles identified with one of the greatest classical dancers, Erik Bruhn! Both as dancer and choreographer, Tetley has moved with facility from ballet to modern and back just as the chief guide to his developing talent, John Butler, has done in a career which has encompassed modern dance, jazz, opera-ballet, Broadway musicals, ice shows, television and the experimental theater.

It is abundantly clear, then, that modern dance has exerted influences of staggering proportions upon ballet enterprise both in America and in Europe. But is the reverse true? Has there been an exchange? Has ballet influenced modern dance? The answer is "Yes," but in more subtle ways.

There had always been one link between ballet and modern and that was to be found in the pre-classic dance forms. Ballet itself had been born of the court dances—of the pavane, the saraband, the gigue and their relatives—and the American modern dance, as it began its first experimentations in the 1920's, recognized the need not only for freedom to invent but also for formal disciplines with respect to choreography. Louis Horst, musician, composer and teacher and a prime influence in Martha Graham's career, found just such disciplines in these same pre-classic dance music sources.

Horst was not concerned with reproducing these ancient forms nor the etiquette (which colored ballet) that went with them. It was the sturdy skeleton in which he was chiefly interested. He exposed Graham herself and his own pupils —four decades of them—to the pre-classic dance forms, and with the possibilities of this artistic skeleton as a control, he led them to express the "now" and to dress it in today's ideas and needs. This, then, was a basic, if distant, link.

Other influences came later. The moderns eschewed elaborate costuming and decor in the twenties and thirties, but by the time the forties rolled in, they took a leaf from the ballet's book and began to return to the trappings, the helpful and often necessary production complements to the dance act itself. Graham was in the vanguard here. Costumes and decor were totally different from that associated with ballet—in settings, for example, the sculptured form was preferred to the flats and drops of the ballet.

Technically, too, the moderns, who had been so concerned

with the articulation of the torso (a major section of the body which they felt ballet had neglected), slowly began to add to their range of movement virtuosities of the legs and feet. They did not execute entrechats—although Graham said she would use them freely if she ever felt she needed to do so—but they found their own equivalents of batterie, of flashing footwork which brings excitement to any form of dance. The moderns also expanded their musical uses to include highly classical examples of traditional music (Bach was

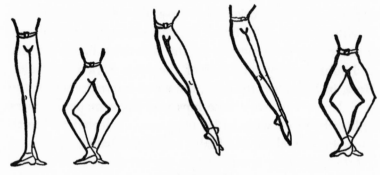

Brisé—Batterie

always a favorite) and to dance, increasingly, themes of romance. Finally, they began referring to their own productions in modern dance as "ballets."

Jazz was destined to influence ballet and, indeed, become a part of it, just as the popular rhythms of earlier times found their way into ballet productions, for folk expression feeds art expression. Today, jazz and its variants constitute a major force in our culture. If the mazurka or the polonaise or even the jota could find new theatrical outlets in ballet, so could jazz.

Robbins's *Fancy Free,* employed folk idioms with respect not only to behavior (that sailors chase girls is most certainly well-established folklore around the world) but also to jazz rhythms. In fact, *Fancy Free* was so close to the popular theater that it seemed only a natural step for its three collaborators—Robbins (choreography), Leonard Bernstein (music), Oliver Smith (design)—to use it as something of a springboard in the creating of a Broadway musical comedy hit, *On the Town.*

With *Interplay,* one of the most popular jazz ballets of the century, Robbins worked in reverse. He created it first for a Broadway show, Billy Rose's *Concert Varieties,* and then saw it move into the repertory of the American Ballet Theatre and subsequently into that of the New York City Ballet. Here, in *Interplay,* the beat, the air of improvisation of the jazz dancer and even loose hips and finger-snappings were brilliantly fused with ballet movements selected for pertinance in the making of a flashy, frolicsome ballet.

Interplay's only quiet section, the pas de deux, also combined, skillfully, blues rhythm and mood with ballet action.

Interplay was created in 1945 and has remained a favorite with audiences in America and abroad ever since. But in 1958, Robbins founded his own company, Ballets: U.S.A., and for it created the enormously successful *N.Y. Export, Op. Jazz,* in which he went even further in blending the brilliant steps of ballet and stunning theatricalisms with the insistent, restless rhythm of jazz.

If Robbins has been the most strikingly successful purveyor of jazz to the ballet world, he is by no means the only one. Anna Sokolow has long worked in the jazz idiom, and although she is a modern dance choreographer, she has created jazz works especially for ballet. In her choreography, it is not simply the jazz beat and the jazz gesture which emerge but also the sullenness, the ferocity and the insecurity of youth in the jazz age itself.

Jazz is by no means a johnny-come-lately to the art of dancing. Long before Robbins and Sokolow, Helen Tamiris, one of the pioneers of America's modern dance, was experimenting with jazz dances in concert dance form. In the 1920's, as the first American to dance at the Salzburg Festival after Isadora Duncan's time, Tamiris introduced the festival's serious concert-goers to serious jazz dance. Since those days, jazz has become more and more of a staple ingredient in choreography for the contemporary theater: for musical comedy, for movies, for modern dance and for ballet.

Another major ballet trend of the twentieth century is found in the increasing popularity of abstract ballets. Balanchine, who is the foremost creator in this idiom, has said that there is no such thing as a truly abstract ballet, since when a male and female confront each other on stage or dance together, drama or incident is present even if only in potential.

Balanchine's great *Serenade* is a perfect example of this, for although it has no story and although its focus is upon the glorious designs which he has devised for soloists, duos, small groupings and full corps, he has exploited this dramatic, or emotional, potential by coloring some of the movements and the gestures, and even the pauses, with suggestions of longing, of finding, of waiting and of losing.

His *Concerto Barocco* (to music of Bach, the double violin concerto) eschews this ever so delicate aura of romance. It is a cool ballet, one which seeks to give movement extension to the rhythm, form and quality of the score. Works of this nature were called, by Denishawn (the company headed by Ruth St. Denis and Ted Shawn), "music visualizations." Perhaps this term best describes those storyless, abstract ballets which are inspired and governed by music.

A list of Balanchine's abstract ballets would be almost endless, for he can seemingly tick them off in a matter of hours. Certainly, *Symphony in C* (Bizet) is a perennial, and there are *Gounod Symphony, Donizetti Variations, Raymonda Variations* (Glazounov), *Allegro Brillante* (Tchaikovsky), *Ballet Imperial* (Tchaikovsky), *Bourrée Fantasque* (Chabrier) with elements of humor, *Divertimento No. 15* (Mozart), *Divertimento* (Haieff), *Four Temperaments* (Hindemith) with its contrasting moods, *Scotch Symphony* (Mendelssohn) and many, many more, including various pas de deux and pas de trois.

These twentieth-century abstract ballets are in striking contrast to the ballets of the nineteenth century: the Romantic Age with its narrative ballets and the Petipa Age with its complex plots (just try to figure out *Raymonda* sometime).

It was hardly surprising that modern Soviet dancers, critics and audiences did not take to the Balanchine abstractions when they were first exposed to them in the 1960's. Where was the plot? the purpose? the conflict? the propaganda? They knew that Balanchine was a product of their own ballet tradition, but at first they could not recognize the fact that he had gone beyond them into a new century while they, in long isolation, were about a half-century behind the rest of the world in matters of choreography (not in performing, since they are dazzling dancers).

Balanchine may have been the leader in the field of abstract choreography but he was certainly never alone.

Fokine's *Les Sylphides* (1908) to music of Chopin (it is often called *Chopiniana*) is an abstract ballet which, however, without telling a story, seeks to capture the essence of the Romantic Age of ballet as it was symbolized in *La Sylphide*. (Balanchine's *Scotch Symphony* is also a tribute to the Scottish fairy-fantasy of *La Sylphide*).

Sir Frederick Ashton, for Britain's Royal Ballet, has been as successful in the making of abstract ballets as he has been in creating his dramatic and poetic masterworks. His *Symphonic Variations* (Franck), *Birthday Offering*, created in honor of the twenty-fifth anniversary of the founding of the Vic-Wells Ballet (then Sadler's Wells, then Royal) *Homage to the Queen* (made for the coronation of Elizabeth II) and other stirring, storyless ballets.

Most of Massine's symphonic ballets had some sort of a plot (such as the Berlioz *Symphonie Fantastique*) or a scheme involving literal characters (Beethoven's *Seventh Symphony*), but the basic idea was music visualization; and of them all, *Rouge et Noir* (Shostakovitch) came closest to achieving this.

Perhaps the principal reason for choreographers' interest in abstract ballets is that they, the choreographers, can create directly for a dancer and not have to go through the process of creating for a dancer who is playing someone else (a character in a dramatic ballet). The choreographer and his dancers, therefore, are instantly and directly linked, and the skills, the styles and, to a degree, the personalities of the dancers can be immediately explored and exploited by the choreographer for artistic goals.

England's Kenneth MacMillan, though seemingly more comfortable choreographically with story ballets, has done some effective work in the abstract ballet area. The American Thomas Andrew finds the abstract ballet, generated by a musical base, most congenial to his choreographic talents (although he is adept with dramatic ballets also), and other young choreographers have turned to this apparently inexhaustible field of abstraction or "pure" dance, that is, dance for the sake of dancing.

Even Robbins, with his flair for drama, has had a go at abstract dance. His delightful *Fanfare* (an American's greeting to England's Elizabeth II at her crowning), set to Britten's "Young Person's Guide to the Orchestra," is a prime example of the Robbins command of dance responses to musical invitations and dictates. It has humor in it and antic actions, but it is not a story ballet.

Robbins's *The Pied Piper* (to music of Aaron Copland) might serve as a good example of the middle ground between story ballet and abstract ballet. The legend of the Pied Piper of Hamlin is not told in this ballet; rather the ballet is a distillation (or an abstracting) of the compulsion to follow, to respond to, to obey, to fight against, to become identified with the lure, the hypnotic powers of music.

For those Americans and western Europeans who still hold to the dated, inaccurate 1890's view that dancing is a trivial art or, at best, a pretty one (Orientals, with their philosophies and faiths made manifest in dance, would never be guilty of this), it would come as a surprise that dance is capable of social and political comment.

The modern dancers were the most active in this area, particularly during the post-World War I period in central Europe and during the American depression of the 1930's. Tamiris protested the plight of the American Negro in her

How Long, Brethren, and she and Graham and Carmelita Maracci had something to say through dance about the fascist rise in Spain's civil war.

Undoubtedly the most famous social comment ballet is the prize-winning *The Green Table,* an antiwar dance-drama created in 1932 by Kurt Jooss for his Jooss Ballet. In it, he conveys, through mimed and danced episodes, the sorrows and the horrors of war, profiteering, greed and the inescapable force of death. The ballet takes its name from the conference table around which masked diplomats meet to continue the idiocies which led to war in the first place.

Jooss's technique in general was a mixture—or, perhaps, compromise is more accurate—of ballet basics and modern dance. Its built-in limitations, its transitional guise, doomed it to a short but effective life. *The Green Table* was the exception.

Actual ballet, however, was also capable of expressing ideas of social comment. Robbins, in his *Guests,* without indicating differences in races or nationalities, projected powerfully the theme of social ostracism, a meaningless ostracism. In his *The Age of Anxiety,* he commented upon those very anxieties which Auden writes of in his book and which Bernstein captured in his score.

The Soviet ballet has, of course, used its ballet for propaganda. *The Red Poppy* is a classic example of this; so also is *The Flames of Paris.* Other and later Soviet ballets have contrasted the heroism of the Russians with the cruelty of the Nazis.

De Mille, even as she holds close to the folk ballet idiom in which she excels, has used the folk medium to project social injustice as she did in her *The Four Marys,* a danced commentary on the biased execution of justice accorded the Negro in the South.

Back as far as 1935, Ninette de Valois's *The Rake's Progress,* based on the Hogarth drawings, invited attention to the horrors of eighteenth-century English prisons. This was social comment as seen in retrospect.

Also in retrospective terms were the political commentaries, the portrait of a revolutionary as depicted in Balanchine's *Tyl Ulenspiegel,* a ballet in which the choreographer characterized Tyl not merely as a prankster but as the liberator of Flanders in the rebellion against Spain. Jean Babilée created a ballet around the same character, but in this instance, the rogue and not the hero was defined. Each choreographer had found his own approach.

Some ballets of social comment are geared to a place and a period and become outmoded once the situation has changed; others, however, can be more universal in concept and thus serve or stir the conscience of any age.

Age and period also affect what is avant-garde, for today's avant-garde, if it is valid and not simply shocking, becomes tomorrow's tradition. In 1906, when Ruth St. Denis bared her midriff and danced in bare feet, she was avant-garde. Isadora, in her loose tunic, dancing to Wagner, was also avant-garde. Today, the bikini is with us and generations of barefoot dancers have come and gone—nudity around the feet and legs or on the stomach level is no longer new.

One does not often think of Balanchine as an avant-gardist, but he is. His *Apollo,* first done in 1928, was avant-garde in the extreme as it gave ballet a new direction and mirrored a fresh viewpoint on neoclassicism. Today, *Apollo* is a classic, not strange at all, but exceptionally beautiful and still fresh.

Balanchine, ever the searcher, has continued his experiments with the avant-garde over the years while at the same time pouring forth his bounty of classical ballets. In 1954, for example, he created a shocker, *Opus 34*, to "movie music" of Arnold Schoenberg. First of all, there were all manner of movement distortions—feet and legs turned in instead of out in traditional ballet style; there were shudders and tremors instead of elegant leg-beats; two figures, dressed in bloody bandages, were unwrapped to reveal not skeletons but the flesh itself, as if the skin had been peeled off; a finale which saw the lights turned not upon the dancers but upon a dazed, shocked audience.

With *Ivesiana* (set to the still avant-garde music of New England's Charles Ives) and with his sections of *Episodes*, Balanchine juxtaposed classicism with excursions into new areas of movement, into the avant-garde.

Herbert Ross, in his enormously successful *Caprichos*, inspired by Goya's commentaries on his own etchings, uses adapted balletic action combined with freshly invented movement to convey the macabre scenes of his work. In the ballet's pas de deux, for example, the long-haired, long-skirted female figure is inert, presumably dead, and she moves, rather like a broken doll, only she is manipulated by her partner.

Ross's *The Maids*, taken from the Genet story, is melodramatic but it is also avant-garde in its exploration of a savage conflict of emotions in which the two maids are danced by two male dancers (a notion indicated by Sartre in his introduction to the Genet work).

Gerald Arpino's *Ropes*, which calls for dancers to move in choreographic patterns while suspended in air, is certainly an avant-garde creation, as is his *Incubus,* which transpires on ground level.

Does the future of ballet lie in the avant-garde? To a degree its does and it must, for ballet can never rest content with its past accomplishments. Camargo shortened her skirt and thus gave new areas of aerial action to the female dancer —that was avant-garde; Taglioni made dancing on pointe not only the rage of the day but a historic necessity for the future —that was avant-garde; Fokine, in 1909, with his whirling, leaping warriors straining at their bows as unseen arrows pierced the air, shook the citadel of ballet, Paris, to its foundations—that was avant-garde; and when Nijinsky, as choreographer, turned in the limbs of his dancers and made them move flatly, as bas-reliefs, in his *Afternoon of a Faun* or as he devised hitherto unseen actions for the then cacophonic sounds of Stravinsky in *Le Sacre du Printemps,* he was in the avant-garde.

The best of today's avant-garde, then, will become tomorrow's ballet tradition, a living tradition which, through the great repertories of ballet companies around the world, will ever represent and honor the romantic, the classical, the dramatic, the modern, the folk, the jazz, the abstract, the avant-garde elements in the challenging and changing, but ever magical, world of ballet.

Chapter 2

The Choreographer

When the dancers, in Jerome Robbins's *Interplay*, hot-footed it down to the footlights so that they were seen only in silhouette, snapped their fingers, caromed their hips from east to west and back again, you could hardly blame conservative dance followers from exclaiming, "How, in heaven's name, did such carryings-on ever get into a ballet?"

In 1945, when it was first created, *Interplay* came as something of a delightful shock. Since it was first given in a revue, one could say, "Oh, well, it was designed for show business." But less than six months after its revue debut it was in the repertory of the American Ballet Theatre, and in 1952 it was added to the repertory of the classical-minded New York City Ballet.

Interplay has indeed become a ballet classic, despite (or maybe because of) loose hips and jazzy rhythms. It is not unique in its use of jazz (Robbins himself had used it earlier in his first big success, *Fancy Free*), but it provides a fine example of how and why jazz ever got into the sacred confines of the ballet in the first place. The answer is simple. Jazz dancing is the American folk dancing of the mid-twentieth century. Folk dancing, social dancing, has always fed the ballet, has indeed provided much of its source strengths and governed its forms since ballet came into incipient being four hundred years ago.

Does a polonaise in a Petipa classic disturb you? Why, then, should a taste of the lindy in a Robbins ballet bother you?

The art of the choreographer has always dealt with the interrelations of dance forms and techniques. Of course, he invents steps and gestures, sequences and designs—much of his art springs from his own uniqueness, his own wellsprings of originality—but he would not be a total artist if he did not mirror in his works the tastes, the substances of his times. And this was true of the choreographer when Louis XIV ruled France and when Louis himself danced in the most elegant and extravagant of his royal ballets.

The choreographer for ballet did not emerge full-blown from the head of Terpsichore. He did not stand, with Olympian authority, before a band of royal and noble folk preparing to take part in a courtly entertainment and say: "Now these are the five positions of the feet which I have invented, this is a plié, we shall also use glissades and pas de bourrées." No, his majesty's designer of amusing or politically important fêtes said no such thing, but he did use such things as pliés and incipient glissades and the like. Where did he find them? In the social dances of his day.

The sixteenth-century choreographer, given a theme on which to create his spectacle, used the court dances, perhaps slightly adapted to serve his plan of presentation, plus pantomime to tell the story, along with music, song, poetry, dramatic declamation and both scenic and costume effects.

For more than two centuries, right into the eighteenth century, the principal dance ingredients in ballet were the social dances of the court: the pavane, the saraband, the gigue, the rigaudon, the passepied, the chaconne, the bourrée, all of them. Such dances, in the beginning, in their origins, had nothing whatever to do with ballet, but when there came a need for theatrical dancing, they became the base of that new form.

In time, as choreographers or stagers improved upon the earliest experiments in ballet, or when the dancers, starting in 1661, became hard-working professionals rather than pleasure-seeking aristocrats, these dances (now referred to as pre-classic dance forms) took on new extensions in matters of technique, of virtuosity.

So it was that although Françoise Prévost, premiere danseuse of the Opéra in Paris in the early 1700's, continued to dance, say a passepied, she danced the passepied as no mere lady of the court could do. By this time, the glides had indeed become glissades, the walkings had turned into pas de bourrées, the positions of the feet (along with the turnout of the limbs from the hips) and of the arms had become defined. The choreographer was no longer limited to what a queen regnant could do with dance steps, for by 1681, when Lafontaine, the first professional female dancer in the Opéra, had become a stage star, he could be inspired and challenged by something new in the theater, "The Queen of the Dance."

Camargo, who succeeded Prévost as the reigning Queen of the Dance, shed her heels and shortened her skirt and transformed the ballerina from a sliding, gliding figure into a magical aerialist. This innovation, of course, affected the choreographer. More changes had to be made in the old dances, further adaptations of courtly measures had to be instituted if the basic materials of ballet were to keep step with the increased prowess of the professional ballet dancer.

Today's choreographer no longer says to his ballerina, "I'm going to create a chaconne for you." But this does not mean that the pre-classic dance forms have completely disappeared from today's ballet. The direct, lineal descendants of the old steps remain at the historic core of ballet technique, and the deportment of dancers in classical ballets echoes the etiquette of these ancient dances of the court.

On occasion, the old names recur, such as in the Balanchine-Stravinsky *Agon*, created in 1957, which actually lists a Saraband, a Galliard, a Branle. Prévost and even Camargo would be terrified by the technical demands present in these very modern versions of very old dances, just as they would be startled (and lost) by that section of Martha Graham's *Dark Meadow* which the choreographer herself refers to in rehearsal (not in printed programs) as "the saraband." In such new dances, the exact steps of the old dances are no longer present, but the qualities, the moods, the colors and even hints of the formal contours remain.

The choreographer's art, over the centuries, grew right along with his capabilities and imaginativeness in constantly extending the basic elements of the court dances into new, more complex and more theatrically exciting actions, in incorporating current and upcoming social dance patterns into the vocabulary of ballet and in linking such historic and popular materials of dance with movements of his own invention.

Ballet did not invent the rigaudon, say, but the rigaudon,

along with its companion forms, helped the choreographers to invent ballet. Later, the ballet could not claim to have devised the czardas, the mazurka, the polka, the polonaise or any such dance forms. Such were created by no one man, for they came from the people themselves as expressions of the folk and the gentry of a given period. The ballet choreographer wisely incorporated them whenever possible into his new theater pieces. To omit popular dances—suitably adapted and refined—from what the choreographer hoped would be a popular stage work would be foolish indeed.

So it was logical that if Prévost excelled in passepieds—a contemporary wrote that "composers write passepieds because Mlle. Prévost dances them with such fluent elegance" —ballerinas of a century later would find great favor with the public in their theatrical treatments of popular dances. Fanny Elssler, for example, was particularly successful in those ballet divertissements which cast her as a Spaniard, a Hungarian, a Pole, a Russian and others in a wide variety of national dances. In fact, her New York debut was made in *La Cracovienne* and *La Tarentule*. Elssler, if she had by no means started the trend of using national dances in ballet productions, had given a fresh impact and a new treatment to the trend when, in 1836, she triumphed dancing a Cachucha, with castanents and all, in a ballet with a Spanish setting, *Le Diable Boiteux*.

Coppélia without its adored Czardas and Mazurka? Unthinkable! And would you eliminate from ballet those colorful national dances around which most of Act III of *Swan Lake* is built? And certainly, Bournonville's *Napoli*, without its rousing Tarantella, would be incomplete.

Ballet's concern with folkloric materials and the stimulation of social dance measures has been a constant in its history. In the old Danish ballet of 1786, Galeotti's *The Whims of Cupid and the Ballet Master*, there are French, Greek, Tyrolean, Quaker, African, Danish and other types of dances inspired by various nationalities. Truthfully, each would be absolutely unrecognizable to the folk in the presumed countries of origin, for their ethnic connections were loose at best.

A later Danish ballet, Bournonville's *Far From Denmark*, was somewhat closer to authenticity, but not much, in its dances about American Indians, Eskimos and other then-exotic creatures. Elssler did better and so did her successors, both ballerinas and choreographers.

At the beginning of this century, it was Michel Fokine who strove to introduce greater ethnic authenticity into ballet. His concern was not with the divertissements—the mazurkas, polkas, etc.—contained in the big Petipa ballets but, rather, with stylistic accuracy of the whole ballet. He rebelled, as we know, against choreography which used exactly the same steps for a fairytale ballet, a ballet using an Egyptian theme or a Greek theme or an Oriental theme. There were, of course, the national dance interpolations, dances in demi-caractère style (for a Harlequin, a Jester, a Gypsy), and there were mime sequences which might mirror different temperaments, but the overall choreographic cast of a ballet of Petipa's period reflected an increasing reliance on a formula which would serve any theme.

Fokine would have none of that. He studied, observed and absorbed the arts and crafts and histories of those lands or peoples whose lore or legends might serve him as choreographic material. As a choreographer of ballet, he was not at all interested in replacing ballet technique with some other dance technique, nor was he bent on transporting folk dance to the stage. All he asked—and it was indeed revolutionary at the turn of the century—was that each ballet would demand

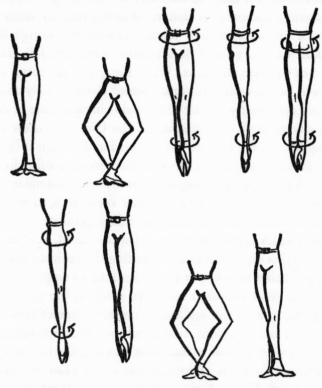

Tour en l'Air (Air Turn)—Single or Double

its own style, that each theme would dictate the manner in which ballet technique would be fused with either the historic or folkloric theme at hand.

Air turns, say, could be used in ballets with Greek, Tartar, Russian, Spanish or Chinese backgrounds, but they would be adapted to the styles and colors associated with the time, the place, the character.

If such use of a classical step in a ballet with ethnic roots seems forced—for Chinese dancers don't do air turns nor does the average Spaniard—it should be noted that air turns are almost a leit motif for Billy himself in Eugene Loring's *Billy the Kid.* Cowboys don't do air turns. American folk dance does not employ air turns. Why, then, use air turns in a Western ballet with a historic theme? Because they mirror strongly and clearly the air of bravado characteristic of Billy or of any showoff. The gunman of the Old West drew fast, he might even flip his gun over in his hand or spin it before firing in a fine display of arrogant fearlessness; Billy, in the ballet, doesn't spin the gun, he spins himself. The movement is true to Billy's character and to the West. It is, in essence, a brilliant theatricalization of a revealing gesture.

Thirty years before *Billy the Kid* was created, Fokine was beginning his experiments in expanding the horizons and the usages of ballet whereby it could continue to employ and to exploit its great technical resources while at the same time enhancing it with the endless colors and characteristics of myriads of races, regions, tribes, cultures and individuals.

Fokine, who did not exclude the fanciful, the romantic or the abstract from his choreographic creed (*Les Sylphides, Le Spectre de la Rose*), shared the fruits of his artistic revolution with other choreographers. Nijinsky, in creating his *Afternoon of a Faun,* found inspiration in ancient Greek bas-reliefs, in hieratic designs. In this ballet, he discarded the turnout of limbs for side-by-side placement of the feet. Indeed, it was a ballet of "sides," for the choreographer endeavored to mirror in his work the flatness of antique reliefs or, perhaps, that flatness which a bright, golden sun can give to a three-dimensional object (ancient Egyptian art reflects this illusionary power of sunlight).

But is this the only way that Debussy's *Afternoon of a Faun* can be choreographed? Certainly not. Nijinsky's *Faun,* created in 1912, represents a romanticized view of antique Greek design while at the same time projecting the eroticism of a mythical creature, half-man and half-animal, as he is stirred to sensual action by the warmth of the sun. In 1953, Jerome Robbins created an entirely new ballet to the same Debussy music and he, too, called it *Afternoon of a Faun.*

The Robbins *Faun* does not take place in a woodland setting, nor does it even nod in the direction of ancient Greece. Its setting is an airy ballet studio with a wall of mirrors (an invisible wall rising over the footlights) such as one would find in any dance studio. There is no dappled Faun here. Instead, there is a young man lying on the floor. He stretches his muscles with pleasure and, as he moves, he watches himself in the invisible mirror—he does not see the audience, but only his own reflection. He tests himself in poses and patterns, ever-watching himself with a sort of cool curiosity.

A girl enters, a ballet dancer (the nymphs of the old *Faun* are not here), and she too focuses her entire attention upon herself as seen in the mirror. The boy, half-man and half-animal but not at all mythical, experiences the sensuality of his own actions. He finds the girl, of course, but in the mirror, and as they move toward each other and, finally, move together, they continue to watch themselves and the patterns they make. Self-scrutiny, essential to the dancer, intermingling with self-love and a total awareness of the body, are the characteristics of the faun and of the nymph which Robbins created from fact and not from myth.

At the close of the Nijinsky version, the Faun, having chased and teased the nymphs, returns to his rock with the scarf that one of the nymphs has dropped. He spreads it out tenderly and then slowly lowers his body upon it in a movement of erotic desire. In the Robbins ballet, the boy kisses the girl tenderly on the cheek, she touches the place with surprised fingertips and withdraws. The youth, the faun, returns to his sensual repose upon the floor.

Both ballets are *Afternoon of a Faun,* though choreographed in totally different styles.

Leonide Massine, who followed Fokine as chief choreographer of Diaghileff's Ballets Russes, was also representative of that new age of choreography which Fokine had launched within the framework of ballet. In his *The Three-Cornered Hat,* Spanish dance is the key ingredient. There are some ballet steps in it and a good deal of movement is Spanish dance adapted to ballet. Still, it is unmistakably a Spanish ballet. In fact, Massine himself was most effective as a Spanish dancer, and his ballet was sufficiently close to authentic Spanish to make it possible for Argentinita herself, one of the greatest of Spanish dancers of the nineteen thirties and forties, to appear in it as guest artist.

With his *Capriccio Espagnol,* Massine actually had Argentinita as his choreographic collaborator. One could hardly say that in his *Le Beau Danube* or *Gaité Parisienne* he turned for inspiration to actual ethnic or folk elements, but he did turn to popular dance forms. In the former he celebrated the Viennese waltz and in the latter, France's popular theatrical dance of the 1890's, the cancan. Massine, who has always leaned toward the application of national themes to ballet, once tried his hand at Americana in a ballet called *Union Pacific,* but in his tale of the building of our transcontinental railroad, one experienced the odd feeling that he was on his way to Omsk or Minsk.

George Balanchine, younger than Massine, was the last truly major choreographer to serve Diaghileff and his Ballets Russes. The name "Balanchine," however, is not immediately associated with ballets which incorporate folk, national or ethnic ingredients. Balanchine always seems to be the purist, working with the materials of classical ballet itself, or original gesture, working them into new, startling and amazingly fresh sequences.

But Balanchine has not dismissed the ethnic, although he has used Russian, Scottish, American, Japanese and other dance colors in his own highly individual way. *Scotch Symphony,* for example, is not really much more Scottish than the old *La Sylphide* with its admixture of folklore and classical steps. Indeed, it is almost a distillation of the elements of *La Sylphide.* What Balanchine has done is to find the balletic equivalents of certain Scottish steps and poses—and let us not forget that Scottish dancing has an elegance of port de bras and of step and stance very closely associated with ballet.

With his version of *Firebird,* Balanchine has turned to Russian folk sources, not for the passages for the glittering, fanciful Firebird herself but, rather, for the Princess and her attending maidens. *Bugaku* has a score by a contemporary Japanese composer, and just as this score contains both Japanese and Western idioms, so too does the Balanchine choreography. He uses the toe shoe of the West but he also introduces the flexed foot of the Japanese dancer. The slow, deliberate pacing is also Japanese, while the lifts which Balanchine has devised for the young man and his betrothed are balletic in base but Oriental in their delicacy.

Balanchine, in his excursions into Americana, also retains his classical approach. Thus, his highly popular *Western Symphony* is fundamentally a classical ballet, but what he has done is to find balletic equivalents to folk steps and gestures, to use grands battements for the high-kicking saloon girls and to brush his actions with the robust colors of the Wild West. He has worked along the same lines in his rousing *Stars and Stripes* in which he has taken Americans' love for parades and patriotic spectacles and re-created elements of this special kind of folklore into balletic terms.

The relating of ballet technique to folk forms was given a real tour de force treatment by Balanchine in his *Square Dance*. In this ballet, the dancers executed steps and formations to the accompanying instructions of an American folk dance caller. Balanchine did not simply settle for the ballet equivalents of star figurations or promenades home or back-to-back. He went further. As an example, one could point to the place where Patricia Wilde (who created the principal role) executed those marvelously difficult gargouillades as the caller shouted, "Now keep your eyes on Pat; her feet go wicketywack!" Such parallels were to be observed throughout the ballet, not slavishly pursued, but found with sufficient frequency to make the point of the parallel and to institute many a chuckle.

But Balanchine, in *Square Dance,* did not stop with paralleling ballet steps with the instructions of the caller. He set the entire affair to music of Corelli and Vivaldi. And it worked! For underlying the music, the calls, the steps of ballet, were the rhythms of dance. The Corelli and Vivaldi measures, with their historic roots in the folk and court dance rhythms of an earlier age, lent their air and cadence to a twentieth-century ballet and to the folk of another time and place with delightful and amusing harmoniousness.

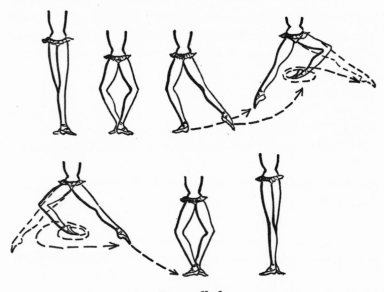

Gargouillade

Agnes de Mille, like Balanchine, uses ballet technique as a basic discipline for her creations, but she goes much further than her precedessors—Fokine, Massine, Balanchine—in exploiting, extending, theatricalizing actual folk materials. In *Rodeo*, in a brief scene before the lowered front curtain, she too uses folk dance calls, but with them she uses authentic folk dance steps. But authentic as they are, they have been patterned and paced and polished by the hand of a master choreographer.

Elsewhere in *Rodeo* (first produced in America in 1942; De Mille had created earlier versions in England in the 1930's), the choreographer fused ballet with folk patterns and, even more important, with folk behavior. The clog was there but so also were fanciful movement conceptions which transformed a dancer into a combination of horse and rider. The prowess of ballet was used to highlight the exuberance of folk spirit, the expansiveness of the American character and the American land.

De Mille has carried this even further in her *The Wind in the Mountains,* a remarkable work in which she seems to synthesize all of her choreographic concepts of dance Americana. There are the space-covering runs of the Western scout and his echoing calls, the flash and dash of the fast-hoofing itinerant peddler, the zip and icy clarity of winter and skating or the gentle fall of rain, strength and tenderness (and, sometimes, a bit of foolishness) in the actions of the women matched with the steel of men of action. In *The Wind in the Mountains,* a male figure soars across the stage in fantastic vaulting turns which only the ballet could achieve, but another male figure slips easily to the ground, presses his ear against the earth to harken for the approach of friend or enemy. These two movement actions seem remote from each other, but as molded by De Mille they are coequal aspects of Americana conceived in theater dance terms.

Drama, based upon emotional conflict and culminating in murder, is the theme of De Mille's *Fall River Legend,* suggested by the Lizzie Borden case. It is an American story to begin with, but it is the drama which is important, so here

"Le Ballet Comique de La Reine," Paris 1581, the first production
to be called a ballet

An early representation of the use of a stage for ballet

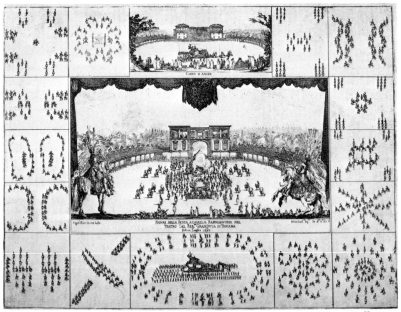

An equestrian ballet spectacle and its choreographic formation,
Italy 1637

Gaetan Vestris, 1729–1808, one of the greatest male dancers of all time

Marie Camargo, 1710–1770, ballerina-innovator in a reproduction of a famous painting by Lancret. *Below:* Marie Sallé, 1707–1756, dramatic ballerina, Camargo's only rival, and the first female choreographer.

Left: Marie Taglioni, 1804–1884, the symbol of the spiritual nature of the Romantic Age of Ballet. *Right:* Fanny Elssler, 1810–1884, Taglioni's only rival, symbol of the earthly nature of the Romantic Age.

George Washington Smith, an American premier danseur who danced with Elssler on her U.S. tour

"Ronzani's Grand Ballet Troupe." Ballet extravaganza comes to America.

"Bayaderka," 1877, choreographed by Petipa to music of Minkus as danced today by Leningrad's Kirov Ballet. *Below:* Spanish Dance in "Swan Lake," danced by Britain's Royal Ballet.

Mira

Vera Fokina and Michel Fokine in "Daphnis and Chloe," an avant-garde ballet in 1912

Left: Anna Pavlova, partnered by Laurent Novikoff in an ethnic-flavored pas de deux. *Right:* Vaslav Nijinsky as the puppet, the title role in the Fokine-Stravinsky "Petrouchka."

The Bolshoi Ballet's Maya Plisetskaya as Kitri in "Don Quixote."
Below: Britain's Royal Ballet, with Donald Macleary and Svetlana
Beriosova in "The Sleeping Beauty."

Mira

The original cast of Jerome Robbins' first ballet "Fancy Free:" Robbins, John Kriza, Harold Lang, Janet Reed, Muriel Bentley. *Below:* "Harbinger," a contemporary American ballet by Eliot Feld, produced by the American Ballet Theatre.

Peter Smith

The Royal Winnipeg Ballet in Brian Macdonald's "Rose Latu-
lippe," a three-act ballet on a Canadian theme: the principal
dancers Annette de Wiedersheim and Richard Rutherford. *Below:*
The Royal Danish Ballet's production of Fokine's "Le Spectre de
La Rose" danced by Niels Kehlet and Solveig Ostergaard.

Mydtskov

Anthony Dowell in Antony Tudor's "Shadowplay" in the repertory of Britain's Royal Ballet. *Below:* Dame Margot Fonteyn and Rudolf Nureyev in Roland Petit's "Paradise Lost," Britain's Royal Ballet.

George Balanchine's "Serenade" (Tchaikovsky) as danced by the New York City Ballet. *Below:* The New York City Ballet's "Movements for Piano and Orchestra" (Stravinsky). Featured, Jacques d'Amboise and Suzanne Farrell.

Edward Villella in his own ballet, "Narkissos," produced by the New York City Ballet

Derbas

Martha Swope

Edward Villella in Balanchine's great classic, "The Prodigal Son," also in the repertory of the New York City Ballet

Dance Collection

Jean Georges Noverre, 1727–1809

Dance Collection

Jean Coralli, 1779–1854

Dance Collection

Auguste Bournonville, 1805–1879

Dance Collection

Marius Petipa, 1822–1910

Michel Fokine, 1880–1942

Maurice Seymour

Leonide Massine, 1894–

Anthony Crickmay

George Balanchine, 1904–

Sir Frederick Ashton, 1906–

Angus McBean

Antony Tudor, 1908–

Agnes de Mille

Jerome Robbins
in his own "Fancy Free"

De Mille has linked ballet movements and ballet's aspects of physical virtuosity with acting, with pantomime (at which de Mille excels). However, the folk element is by no means missing in a dance-drama which the choreographer wished to pinpoint to the American scene itself. The tormented Lizzie, before she succumbs to the inexorable drive to escape from her vicious stepmother and weakling father by chopping them up with an ax, has visions of young people, boys and girls, laughing and romancing together. This is fantasy and choreographed as such. But the prayer-meeting, the church social, bring De Mille back to an exposition of American folk behavior in a ballet which is not expressly regional (New England) Americana but which must be unmistakably American.

But what of the American choreographer whose theme calls for the more distant—exotic, in the exact sense of the word—magic and mystery of the American Indian. Ballet, of course, is prepared to work magic upon the beholder, through the glittering vocabulary of ballet, but only the Indian's age-old steps and stances, forms and figures can evoke the mystery, or the very special mystique, of a unique figure in American culture, the Indian.

Donald Saddler, in his ballet *Koshare* for the Harkness Ballet, has not settled for feathers, tomtoms and war paint nor, on the other hand, has he rejected ballet. How to find a link between the moccasin-shod Indian, moving silently, and the toe shoe, hard and sometimes confining, of the ballerina? The pointe is not used in *Koshare* by Indian maidens—this would be not only an ethnic but also an esthetic violation of a choreographic work rooted in a specific culture—but the pointe is employed by, and appropriate to, the Spider

Woman, a fanciful, fantastic creature; for the use of dancing on toe separates the real from the dream, the known from the unknown, the norm from the magical, just as a sacred mask or a ceremonial costume would do.

In ballets such as *Koshare*, the choreographer needs to possess knowledge of folklore, discernment of the distinctions between fact and legend and, above all, taste. *Koshare's* composer, an American Indian (Louis Ballard), neither duplicated the traditional music of his people nor did he desert it. In composing for the theater, it was his aim to capture the echo of ancient rhythms, timbres and tonalities while making use of a musical sophistication which was universal.

Thus Mr. Saddler could and should use the marvels of pointe dancing for his Spider Woman, a creature of remarkable powers, but he could not do the same for his humans. It was unnecessary to duplicate tribal steps, however, but simply to employ the fundamentals of Indian step and pose and rhythm as a springboard for theater, for danced theater.

Then there are ballets which derive their inspirations and find their movement styles not so much in ethnic sources or rural folk customs as in the popular dances or the etiquette or the fashion of a period. The Tango in Frederick Ashton's *Façade* is not only a satire on the greasy-haired, overardent, near-gigolo type of a long-gone era; it is also a spoof on the temptation to transform the Tango into a rhythmic approach to seduction, involving violent backbends and daring proximities of faces and limbs.

Ruth Page, in the rough and tough and wonderfully honest *Frankie and Johnny* ballet which she choreographed with her long-time associate Bentley Stone, represents not only a ribald fashion in dress but also fashion in movement for a period and a place in which vitality and vulgarity were exuberant playmates. The key to the style? The bawdy old ballad itself.

Bursts of bawdiness with touches of contrasting propriety, also based on time and place, are to be found, say, in Todd Bolender's *Souvenirs,* a ballet set in a resort hotel in the early part of this century. Here, Bolender incorporated the ballroom (or tea dance) steps of the day with the contrasting behavior of such guests as a bride and groom, a masher, a vamp, three wallflowers and . . . well, they are all there. movement techniques derived from ballet were used judiciously and cleverly to enhance or distort, as the case may be, or even comment upon the activities of transients in search of relaxation, fun and adventure amid the potted palms of a hotel lobby.

Lew Christensen's *Filling Station* is of the same genre; that is, there is no folk nor ethnic dancing in it, but it is unmistakably American in its caricaturing of American comic strip characters: the handsome filling station attendant, the tough but friendly truck drivers, the henpecked tourist and his blowsy wife and spoiled brat, the inebriated society girl and her escort and, of course, a gangster, ultimately caught by a state trooper. The relating of ballet technique to this theme is accomplished in several ways, sometimes by combining acrobatics and antics with ballet steps or using a swatch of, say, the Big Apple. But perhaps the best example of the linking of a character and ballet technique is when the filling station attendant (his name is Mac, of course), asked by travelers for directions, goes over to a big map and explains the way by pointing with an extended leg, turning and using port de bras to indicate the routes.

Ruthanna Boris's *Cakewalk* is just as American as *Filling Station*, but here period dance steps (the cakewalk), a theater form (the minstrel show) and American humor conveyed in pantomime and dance (the scenes of the Wallflower or of Hortense, Queen of the Swamp Lilies) are juxtaposed to numbers which are thoroughly balletic while at the same time in keeping with the spirit of such a show (Sleight of Feet and Freebee in their very titles suggest how ballet technique was colored for the needs of this danced Americana).

There are, then, as there have been on an increasing scale for hundreds of years, many ballets which not only mirror the folk of various cultures, lands and regions, but which also draw actual movements from dance folklore itself.

Russian ballet has dug into its ethnic heritage to create ballets of lore and of legend; so too have the Royal Danes (beginning way back in the Bournonville era) with ballets incorporating Danish folk scenes and steps and tales. The English, the Australians (there are ballets based on the rituals of the aborigines), the Mexicans, and on and on. Today's wise choreographer is turning more and more to the still not fully tapped folklore of his country and finding fresh nourishment and new inspiration in those popular dances which are being born every year. The Twist has long since found its way into ballet—not lifted from the dance floor but, rather, adapted for the theater to give, literally, a contemporary twist to a modern ballet.

Jerome Robbins, who related jazz and ballet to such stunning effect in both *Fancy Free* and *Interplay,* never felt that he had plumbed all the riches of jazz. Naturally, not all of his creations have been jazz-derived or jazz-splashed, but when he has created a work with contemporary American purpose, especially involving youth, he has gone even further with his relating of jazz to ballet. A classic in this area is his *N.Y. Export, Op. Jazz.* The movements are derived from popular ballroom dances theatrically heightened by the disciplines of ballet, and with these elements are dashes of humor, bursts of physical exuberance, touches of restlessness, a thread of uncertainty, all of them woven into a choreographic design depicting today's adolescent as he moves to the compulsive beat of today's jazz, to a rhythm close to his own heart, a heart beating faster in a faster age.

Ballet? Of course it is. Prévost, ballerina, had her passepieds, and they are still threaded into the web of ballet. Today's ballet star may be asked to move with the sharp, pulsating insistence of jazz, and that too, one day, will become a part of the very permanent fabric of classical theatrical dancing, ballet.

Chapter 3

The Composer—the Librettist

Music and the dance. What an amiable pair they seem to be! But not always. During the latter half of the nineteenth century and into this, composers barely tolerated the ballet. Composers of grand opera, the theater form which succeeded ballet in popularity during this period (for the first half of the nineteenth century, ballet had dominated opera), were forced by convention to compose music for a ballet within an opera. In almost every instance they grudgingly complied and wrote music which was little better than doggerel.

Gluck had written superb music for ballet, as beautiful as he did for the human voice, but in his era, ballet was honored. It was later that ballet in opera was treated harshly. How strange the transition! There was a time when audiences riveted their attention upon the ballet and chatted or promenaded during the singing of an opera, yet only a few years later, the reverse would be true. The prima donna had replaced the prima ballerina, and the audience used ballet time for forays into the foyer.

Even as late as the 1950's a distinguished editor of a world-famous music publication, when soliciting an essay on ballet, referred to dance as "a minor art." He was, of course, living in the wrong part of the last century. He had forgotten that dance dominated music in an earlier day and that, by the mid-1900's, a renascent dance was not only co-equal with music but, indeed, had inspired some of the major musical scores of the new century.

Cycles in art, as in climate and in culture, are inescapable. Ballet, in its incipiency, was founded not only upon the steps but, of course, upon the music of pavanes, galliards, passepieds, gigues and their many relatives. These were compositions which had their roots in pre-classic dance forms. But later, when composers extended their horizons to move from the suite, which in Bach's day included bourrées and gigues and the like, to the sonata and to the symphony, they seemed to forget that dance was not only the mother-source but also something of the father-form of these historic innovations.

In antiquity and in the arts-expression of non-Occidental theater, music and dance were never isolated one from the other. Sometimes there would be a common term for both, just as in India the term "natya" means dance and drama, inseparably one. In ancient Greece, poetry, unison singing voices, and instruments accompanied movement for both acting and dancing, and the emergence of the "choregos" as the leader of the chorus signified the dual role of choreographer-composer.

With the coming of ballet as a special form of entertainment, dance and music were almost like twins. In the banquet-fêtes which heralded the coming of ballet in the 1400's and 1500's, the harp, as it had been in the days of David, served to accompany both song and dance. There were drums, perhaps the oldest of musical instruments and an ageless source of accompaniment for dancing; and in the elaborate court spectacles of the Renaissance, one would have heard violins, pipes, certain of the wind instruments and vocal dance music.

Villagers and courtiers, the rustic and the refined, made their own music and danced to it.

The close kinship of dance and music was to continue right into the establishing of ballet as a professional theater activity. Louis XIV, who commanded the creation of the Royal Academy of Dancing in Paris in 1661, a decade later appointed Jean-Baptiste Lully as the director and Pierre Beauchamp as the ballet master of the dual-directed academy, l'Académie Royale de la Musique et de la Danse.

Today, we think of Lully as one of the most important composers of his age. He was. But he was also a dancer. In fact, he had come from Italy (his name was Lulli) to the French court as a dancer and violinist and, on more than one occasion, danced in ballets with the King himself.

Lully, of course, composed many operas and the scores for ballets. He also collaborated with the great poets and dramatists, such as Racine and Molière, by writing music for them. But these musical duties in no way obscured his dance origins nor his continuing concern for ballet. It would not seem surprising to us that Beauchamp, a dancer, should dance in a Molière work, but what of Lully? He danced in *Le Mariage Forcé* in 1664 with Beauchamp.

Such was Lully's versatility that he served not only as director of the Académie Royale but also as conductor and stage manager! Lully, then, danced with and composed for Louis. He danced with his ballet master Beauchamp, and he presided over a momentous period in dance when ballet became more than a courtly pastime, when it became professional, when it developed, through the opportunities and disciplines provided by the academic principle, into a serious and responsible art expression. It was here, under Lully, that Beauchamp, an accomplished dancer (his pirouettes were said to be brilliant), firmly established the basic (and unchanging) five positions of the feet, positions which had been in use but which Beauchamp named, described and made an essential starting area for flights of virtuosity.

Two Rameaus, who made their separate but related impacts as the seventeenth century slipped into the eighteenth, were Pierre Rameau (the French dancing teacher who wrote *The Dancing Master,* a book which set down the social dance steps and styles of the early 1700's as well as indicating their relationships to the actions of stage dancing) and Jean Philippe Rameau (composer of opera, ballet and opera-ballet and a distinguished successor to Lully).

Les Indes Galantes, an elaborate opera-ballet produced in 1735, was revived in Paris two centuries later as interest, both in America and in Europe, turned more and more to the music of Rameau. *Les Fêtes d'Hebe* was another popular Rameau opera-ballet, for the composer, although he wrote many operas which contained more song than dance, possessed a profound respect for the art of dancing. He lived, observed and composed during that period when ballet changed from being chiefly a terre-à-terre affair (always for the danseuse) to an aerial art (released by La Camargo into a new area of leaps and jumps).

Today's dance student can study Rameau's scores and, by listening to those passages (and passepieds!) which he composed especially for ballet, learn a great deal about the nature and the flavor, the forms and the rhythms of ballet in the 1700's. And today's music student will learn that, in the works of Rameau, dancing was more than of incidental concern, that the pre-classic dance forms still played solid roles in the structure of music as well as of choreography.

The mid-1700's was not a time for standing still in either music or dance. Rameau expressed his interest in the ballet reforms demanded by and instituted by Jean Georges Noverre. Noverre, with his ballet d'action, wanted the art to be expressive and not merely physical (Camargo's leaps, though lovely, were not quite enough for the new age of ballet). Another composer, one who was also a rebel-innovator in music, found himself in full accord with Noverre—he was the great German musician, Christoph Wilibald Gluck. If Noverre remade ballet, Gluck remade opera.

Gluck's interest in dance was profound, and the music he composed for it represented some of the most incandescent creations he or any other composer ever achieved. Noverre wanted the movements of dance to have meaning—to establish character, to reveal situation, to forward the plot. Gluck wanted opera to be cohesive—song, instrumentation, drama, dance all working not sequentially but together.

Gluck, of course, retains his musical hold on the public to this day, particularly through his operas *Orpheus and Eurydice* and *Alcestis,* and it would be impossible to think of them (or even to present them) without dancing as an essential ingredient. So important is dancing to *Orpheus* that in one of Alicia Markova's last appearances at the old Metropolitan Opera House, the critics (music critics) focused their praise upon the ballet aspects of the Gluck masterwork and upon Markova's art.

With the start of yet another century, the nineteenth, ballet turned its sights more and more upon the drama of dance. Noverre's concept of "action ballet" found continuation not only in such works as Dauberval's *La Fille Mal Gardée* (1786), the most famous comedy classic in all ballet, but also in Salvatore Vigano's "choreodrammas," among them, *The Creatures of Prometheus* (for which Beethoven wrote the score), first produced in 1801.

The dramatic ballet, then, needed musical accompaniments which were far more than incidental music to incidental dances or formal musical backgrounds to standard dance forms. The force, the thrust, the dynamic range of symphonic music was required along with leit motifs of sound capable of reflecting leit motifs in the course of a dance drama.

The Romantic Age of ballet, beginning with Marie Taglioni's triumphant performance in *La Sylphide* in Paris in 1832, would be one in which musical and movement themes would become more closely wedded for dramatic ends than ever before. Adolphe Adam's score for *Giselle* (1841) is a perfect example of this. We have, today, no exact choreographic record of what Coralli and Perrot created, since the ballet was passed on by memory to succeeding generations of performers, and many changes most certainly have been made; but the Adam music remains in full, and its sounds are marvelous guides to the steps, gestures, moods and dramatic surges of one of the greatest dramatic ballets of all time. Listen, and you will hear Giselle's gentle theme, a happy leit motif which will recur subsequently, with distortions, for the Mad Scene. Albrecht has his dashing theme and Hilarion his crude, noisy, angry one. The Wilis are omened in music, and the score itself clearly underlines scenes varying from playfulness to dramatic confrontation, from courtship to deep remorse, from the lilt of peasant dancing to the dark, brooding, fearful atmosphere of witchcraft. Adam's score for *Giselle* is almost a choreographed score.

Other ballets of the Romantic Age—*La Sylphide*, of course, included—pursued similar patterns in integrating the drama of music with the drama of dance.

The term "choreographed score" used above is by no means far-fetched, for ballet was moving to yet another era in which choreographers would literally tell the composer what to write and how to write it.

The Viennese composer Ludwig (or Leon) Minkus served as staff composer first at Moscow's Bolshoi Theater and subsequently at the Maryinsky in St. Petersburg. During his more than thirty years in Russia (ending in 1886), he composed an impressive number of ballets, many of them full-length and several of them destined to become classics. A swift and facile writer of music, he had, it was reported, a large backlog of dances carefully filed as to forms, rhythms and national colors (Spanish, Oriental, etc.), so that when the choreographer, say it was Petipa, called for a new score with certain specifications, Minkus could dip into his files of previously composed music and come up with many pieces suitable for inclusion in the new composition.

Don Quixote, a permanent full-length favorite in the repertories of Russian ballet troupes for a century, has lent its Grand Pas de Deux to the whole world, and its tunes are so catchy that one leaves the theater humming them. Another Petipa-Minkus masterpiece is *La Bayadère,* which the ballet public outside the Soviet Union has come to admire and to love.

Minkus music constitutes a superb base for choreography. It may not be hailed as great music, and often it is unabashedly corny, but it gives the right beat at the right time, the right colors for shifting scenes and moods, and airs which please the ear. Many a student dancer has been told by his instructor, "If you can't keep time to Minkus, forget a dance career." Indeed, it is impossible *not* to keep time to the clearcut, uncluttered, forceful rhythms of one of the last century's most important ballet composers.

Peter Tchaikovsky was also a composer of ballets, succeeding Minkus in serving the Russian Imperial Ballet. Tchaikovsky happened to be a far greater composer, one who did not need ballet to achieve international fame. But Tchaikovsky, on commission, did compose expressly for ballet and turned out three immortal scores for the art of dancing: *The Sleeping Beauty, The Nutcracker* and *Swan Lake.*

Tchaikovsky also submitted to the exact and exacting orders of the choreographer and turned out, on demand, mazurkas, polonaises, czardases, Spanish dances, tarantellas or tinkly music (for the Christmas tree lighting in *Nutcracker*) or Minkus-like boom-boom music for the so-called Black Swan or a haunting adagio for the Swan Queen. Tchaikovsky, then, was called upon to compose "music by the yard" for ballet, but the restrictions seemed to challenge his genius; he did not settle for mere competence in composing music for the dance.

As a matter of fact, the first production of *Swan Lake* (in

Moscow in 1877) was a flop, and the composer died believing that it was *he* who had failed (after his death, a new production of *Swan Lake* with choreography by Petipa and Ivanov transformed a failure into a triumph).

The initial failure of *Swan Lake* had not been Tchaikovsky's fault, although the score had been characterized as "too symphonic." In fact, the score baffled the ballerina, who apparently could not count the beats for dance purposes. It was she who introduced other music for her own variations —perhaps music of Minkus, whose beat she couldn't miss! The choreographer, Julius Reisinger, as well as the ballerina were not first rate, so *Swan Lake* had to wait until 1895 to make its mark as, perhaps, the most popular classical ballet in the entire world.

Tchaikovsky's non-ballet scores have also held the kernels of dance within them. His *Serenade for Strings*, as choreographed by George Balanchine and called simply *Serenade* (created in 1935), as I have pointed out, has thus been identified with a work which is a twentieth-century model of the art of the abstract ballet. Leonide Massine, in 1933, created the first of his historic series of Symphonic Ballets, *Les Présages*, to Tchaikovsky (Fifth Symphony). In the ensuing decades, more and more of Tchaikovsky's music has inspired major choreographers (Balanchine especially) to create ballets of great popularity and enduring significance, both abstract and dramatic, from the dance purity of *Theme and Variations* (Suite No. 3 in G) to the intensely theatrical tone poems of *Francesca da Rimini* and *Hamlet*.

The Russian Imperial and State Ballets have never lacked for composers, great or pedestrian. If it had a Minkus, it also had a Tchaikovsky; if it settled for the services of a Drigo, it also could claim the artistries of a Glazounov (*Raymonda*) or Rimsky-Korsakoff (*Coq d'Or,* an opera-ballet).

The ballet, in Delibes, had a composer of the first rank for the bewitching *Sylvia,* the effervescent *Coppélia* and other ballets; and the international ballet, inside of Russia, in western Europe and in America, could claim in part for its own uses the towering musical genius of the twentieth century, Igor Stravinsky.

Three of Stravinsky's greatest scores were composed expressly for ballet and were produced during a period which just barely exceeded three years. They were *Firebird* (1910), *Petrouchka* (1911) and *Sacre du Printemps* (1913). Nearly half a century later, the great old musical master produced yet another masterwork for ballet, *Agon.* In between, and even after, Stravinsky composed immortal scores especially for ballet (*Apollo,* 1928, and *Orpheus,* 1948, among many).

In addition to his ballet scores, Stravinsky's music invited choreographic responses. Not only has Balanchine, Stravinsky's long-time friend and associate, found inspiration for dance in the composer's non-balletic scores, but so also have other choreographers, among them Jerome Robbins, whose powerful and terrifying *The Cage* is brilliantly mated with Stravinsky's Concerto Grosso in D for Strings.

Stravinsky never stopped being avant-garde. Oh, yes, he composed scores which were classic in contour or lyrical in an almost traditional sense or even frankly nostalgic; in this last category falls the ballet *Le Baiser de la Fée,* Stravinsky's musical tribute to Tchaikovsky. *Sacre,* when it was first done, was a shocker. The near riot it caused at its Paris premiere actually drove the composer from the theater. It is still, more than fifty years later, not only an intensely original work but also avant-garde as a score for ballet.

Agon finds Stravinsky continuing as an up-to-the-minute modernist, an innovator at eighty years of age. But what especially fascinates the dance follower is that the *Agon* score, though extremely modern and filled with Stravinsky's dry and brittle sounds, sardonic wit and zestful surprises, has its roots in those very forms which gave birth to ballet itself: the galliard, the saraband, the branle. The beats are much more difficult to count than those of Rameau in his pre-classic dance form adaptations, but the rhythms, and what is more important, the flavors and the characteristics of these ancient music-dance forms, are present in this very modern music.

Balanchine, in his choreographic treatment of Stravinsky's music, went right along with the composer. The steps and the gestures are those of mid-twentieth-century ballet, technically advanced and highly sophisticated, yet here, renewed for our era, are the marvelous colors, the rhythmic intent and the intrinsic styles of these various forms of old court and peasant dances.

The names of Stravinsky and Balanchine are almost inseparable in our minds today, for the two have worked in close collaboration for so long and with such tremendous success. The two have enormous respect for each other, and since Balanchine's own background is rooted in music (he is both a pianist and a conductor as well as an avid scholar and researcher in music), he can work with Stravinsky with far more than instinct to support him in his discussion of the elements necessary to a new ballet score.

But preceding Balanchine in the dance aspects of Stravinsky's career were other dance leaders of towering proportions: Fokine (*Firebird, Petrouchka*), Nijinsky (*Sacre du Printemps*), Massine (a second staging of *Sacre, Pulcinella*), Nijinska (*Les Noces*) and many more. Even after his long association with Balanchine began, other choreographers have worked successfully with Stravinsky's music, Ashton among them. And how many choreographers, known and unknown, have taken a whirl at *L'Histoire du Soldat,* one of Stravinsky's most famous pieces of music and one which almost defies successful staging.

Stravinsky works closely with the choreographer even after a score is completed. During ballet rehearsals, he is often to be found huddled with Balanchine in a continuing series of consultations, or he will look in on a new production, as he did with the Santa Fe Opera, of his remarkable ballet-oratorio-drama (originally commissioned by the great mime, Ida Rubenstein), *Persephone,* to give his approval of or suggestions to Vera Zorina, the actress-dancer, or to the young choreographer Thomas Andrew.

Not every composer works like Stravinsky. There are as many methods of collaboration between choreographer and composer as there are varying artistries and personalities.

But in any such collaboration, the selection of, or agreement on, a theme would be the primary consideration.

Where do ballet themes come from? Before exploring the relationship of music and choreography, an essential digression is in order, and that has to do with the librettist whose "book" provides a ballet with its theme and whose theme inspires the composer to compose and the choreographer to choreograph.

The historic importance of the book is clearly indicated in an expression still frequently heard, for even laymen ask, "How do you write a ballet?" What they really mean is, "How is a ballet choreographed?" For choreography is wordless (although spoken or sung words may, on occasion, provide an accompaniment or be used in a synthesis of performing arts).

The author of the book, however, was long a major figure in the making of a ballet, an artist coequal to the choreographer, composer, designer. Just take a skim through Cyril Beaumont's monumental work of research, *Complete Book of Ballets* (it begins with a ballet produced in 1786 and runs through 1936, with a peek at early 1937), and you will find "book" by reading the list of credits for almost every ballet contained in this great volume.

The librettists—who are they? Poets, critics, painters, good writers and hack writers have all turned out ballet librettos. Composers also have prepared books for ballets, but the most common librettist is, of course, the choreographer himself.

By "book" for a ballet, we do not necessarily mean the actual source material, even if it stems from a literary masterpiece. Thus, a ballet based on *Faust* will not credit either Goethe or Marlowe, say, with the book, any more than Fokine's *Don Juan* credits the book to Byron, for it is the individual who adapts a classical story, utilizes a poetic theme or originates a plot, situation or incident who is credited with the ballet's "book."

In *Giselle*, for example, it was the poet and great leader of the Romantic Movement in the arts, Théophile Gautier, who actually came across the theme which was to be the base of one of the world's greatest ballets. Gautier read of the legend of the Wilis in a work written by the great German poet Heinrich Heine. Vernoy de Saint-Georges, a professional librettist for many ballets, adapted Gautier's idea to the needs of stage productions, and Jean Coralli, the choreographer of *Giselle* (Jules Perrot, husband of Carlotta Grisi, the first Giselle, arranged her dances for her), took part in molding the book to his choreographic plans. *Giselle,* therefore, credits its book to Gautier, Saint-Georges and Coralli.

Fokine was responsible for the books of several of his own ballets, but in others he either collaborated on a book or worked from one created by another artist: the book for *Scheherazade* is by the Russian painter Alexandre Benois; Stravinsky's *Firebird* by Fokine alone, but Stravinsky's *Petrouchka* by the composer himself and Benois; *Thamar* by another great Russian painter, Leon Bakst, and so it went. The term "book" does not necessarily mean that the ballet is a dance-drama or tells an elaborate story. Fokine is credited with the book for his own *Carnaval,* yet this ballet is little more than a suite of dances involving, it is true, such traditional figures as Columbine and Harlequin. There is passing incident, perhaps, but no cumulative plot.

Stravinsky and Nicholas Roerich (the painter) together wrote the book for the Diaghileff Ballets Russes' celebrated production of *Sacre du Printemps,* and Stravinsky alone provided the book for the young Balanchine's (1928) *Apollo.* In later years, the two great collaborators ignored "book." They discussed themes and ideas, but no formal credits for "book" were necessary; yet *Orpheus* was as much of a book ballet as the much earlier *Apollo. Agon,* of course, had no book and needed none, since it was an abstract ballet, without story, just as Fokine's romantic *Les Sylphides* of fifty years earlier was a plotless, "bookless" ballet.

In the mid-twentieth century, the "book" for ballet went out of fashion, particularly in America. It was understood that the choreographer of a ballet used his own ideas for a theme or dramatic base or adapted any literary work (from the genius of a Shakespeare in *Romeo and Juliet* to the genius of a Hemingway in *Capital of the World*) to suit his own choreographic vision. The choreographer did not feel that he needed a literary middle-man.

The same did not hold true of Europe, particularly in France, where the tradition of the librettist was firmly established and where an odd (to modern-day dance thinking) law made it possible to copyright a ballet libretto but *not* a ballet's choreography.

(A similar inequity has prevailed in America, where choreography has been legally plagiarized for many years and where courts of justice have yet to determine whether ballets recorded in Labanotation or described verbally in minute detail are covered by copyright law or whether only the notational record and the literary record are protected by copyright.)

Aside from France, England did not dispense with the librettist entirely. Ballet librettists had their occasional opportunities. But in the main, the "book" credit disappeared, although book ballets continued to be created by "literate" choreographers. Balanchine's dominance in American ballet in the 1940's, 1950's and 1960's and his vast repertory of "pure" ballets, music visualizations without narrative, obviated the necessity of a librettist since no book was employed.

When Balanchine elected to do a dramatic work (some were such large-scale creations as his new *Nutcracker, A Midsummer Night's Dream* or *Don Quixote*), the choreographer was his own librettist. And other American companies, laying more stress on works with dramatic themes, simply presumed that the book was an inextricable part of the choreography and that the choreographer was responsible for both. There was no need, then, to give special credit to the "book" of a ballet.

With the theme of the ballet determined, the choreographer and the composer are ready for their next step in their collaboration. Usually, the choreographer tells the composer how long he wants the ballet to run, for only he knows how much time is needed for the fulfillment of his choreographic ideas. Furthermore, he is likely to conceive his projected ballet in terms of scenes, movements or episodes or, possibly, short contrasting dances. These factors give the composer guidelines without inhibiting him and his own creative inclinations.

From time to time, adjustments can be made and often are. The composer, say, may come upon a musical theme which takes longer to develop than the choreographer had envisioned for a given piece of choreography. Here, the two creators adjust, compromise. If one must prevail, it very probably should be the choreographer, since the public will eventually be attending a ballet, a dance production, and not a musical concert.

The essential dominance of the choreographer may offend the musician or those of musical bent, but it is an esthetic fact that, in ballet, music must serve dance. Attesting to the validity of this viewpoint is a remarkable young artist, James

Clouser, who is both a choreographer and a composer. Although he has displayed multiple talents as ballet master, a principal dancer, choreographer and composer for the internationally successful Royal Winnipeg Ballet of Canada, Clouser is by no means a dilettante; rather is he the Renaissance man returned to fashion. Just as other choreographers have assumed the duties of the librettist, he has assumed the duties of the composer also (and, on occasion, the designer).

With extensive musical training at the Eastman School of Music behind him, Clouser is not a johnny-come-lately to musical composition. He has composed scores not only for ballets (for the Royal Winnipeg and other troupes) but also for television and for strictly musical performers. In the unique position of being his own collaborator, he can hardly be accused of bias, yet he says that if there is an insoluable conflict between music and dance, dance must come first. He feels, however, that a defeat for one or the other is rare, that adjustments and compromises can almost always be reached.

But he feels strongly that composing for dance and composing music for its own sake require different approaches and that both have to do with form. "In composing for dance, the music must *find* its form within the needs of the ballet; in composing music for its own sake, the music *creates* its own form."

Any composer for ballet must find his way within the proposed form, the choreographic shape, of the ballet itself. On occasion, this might possibly prove to be an onus, but most contemporary composers find the demands themselves to be sources of inspiration as well as simple structural guides.

The choreographer may not only request music of certain length divided into certain acts, scenes or movements and subdivided into specific dances, but may also wish to go a step further and ask for specific rhythms or time signatures at key (to him) spots in his ballet.

The degree to which a composer follows the choreographer's instructions vary considerably, as I have indicated. One composer told me that a certain celebrated choreographer had given him such a detailed breakdown of the dance to be done that "I found myself not merely with a choreographic blueprint but actually with a score that had everything in it but notes!"

In other instances, the choreographer is content with giving the composer a synopsis of his plan, including plot (if any), style and period, and from there on in, the composer has carte blanche. Subsequently, the choreographer sets his steps, gestures, patterns of action and sequences to the score which has been given to him.

How do composers feel about writing music for dancing? Those who can compose music suitable for dance are invariably grateful for the opportunity. William Schuman, composer, teacher, lecturer, administrator, one-time president of the Juilliard School of Music and later president of New York City's Lincoln Center for the Performing Arts, has composed scores for both ballet and modern dance. With honest practicality, he points out that his music receives far greater exposure, many more performances, if it is part of a dance production than if it is exclusively symphonic or chamber music. Symphony audiences—and this is hardly a secret—prefer the classics to novelties, and the contemporary composer gets short shrift when pitted against a Beethoven or a Brahms. Conductors strive to introduce new works and to play creations by contemporary composers, but the box office shows who draws steadily.

Dance is different. The audience goes not for the music but for the ballet itself. So it is that Aaron Copland's score for Agnes de Mille's *Rodeo* and his music for Martha Graham's modern dance masterpiece, *Appalachian Spring*, have had far greater exposure than his compositions designed only for orchestra.

Prokofieff knew that the theater brought his art to the attention of more persons than did the concert hall. It was not lack of invention that caused him to use a portion of his *Classical Symphony* in his score for the ballet of *Romeo and Juliet;* he simply wanted more people to hear this music!

There are still, in the late twentieth century, hack composers attracted to jobs with dance, both ballet and modern, but in the main, the renascent art of dancing has invited the collaboration and attendant enthusiasm of some of the world's greatest composers. In this area, modern dance has had the edge over ballet, for Martha Graham alone has commissioned major musical works by Copland, Schuman, Dello Joio, Hindemith, Barber, Menotti, Chavez, Surinach, El-Dabh and many others. Indeed, Graham herself has been honored by the musical world for her vast contribution to contemporary music through the commissioning and worldwide performing of new scores.

But ballet need not hang its head. It has had the gigantic services of Stravinsky and Prokofieff in recent years along with the valued contributions of slightly lesser talents.

Ballet, however, finds musical support far beyond those scores especially commissioned for dance. The vast repertory and repository of musical compositions are, with a few notable exceptions (the Ravel estate will not permit dancers to use any of Ravel's music except that expressly written for theater), available to choreographers. Occasionally, there has been the inevitable hue and cry from musicians, but this has become rare since the 1930's when Massine created his symphonic ballets and caused a furor in musical circles.

Long before Massine, the rebellious genius Isadora Duncan had refused to dance to doggerel composed for the deadly ballets of the late nineteenth century and had used the works of Gluck (not simply his ballet music), Chopin, Wagner and other musical masters as springboards for her highly personal dance expressions.

Massine's symphonic ballets—*Les Présages* (Tchaikovsky), *Choreartium* (Brahms), *Symphonie Fantastique* (Berlioz), *Seventh Symphony* (Beethoven's so-called Dance Symphony), *Rouge et Noir* (Shostakovitch)—broke the resistance of rigid musical purists and made it possible for any suitable music to serve as "the floor" of dance, as Balanchine has described it.

Balanchine himself, more than any other choreographer, has exploited non-dance music for ballet ends extensively and successfully. His choreographic genius has rarely failed to do honor to music ranging from that of Tchaikovsky and Stravinsky through Mozart and Mendelssohn to Webern and Ives. Never is he guilty of violating musical intent; mostly, he extends music into another dimension, giving it visual form as counterpart to its aural life.

The choreograhper is limited in his treatment of non-dance music only by disciplines demanded by the music and by taste. Balanchine, for example, employs no story, no passion, no emotional incident in his *Concerto Barocco* (to Bach's double violin concerto); in *Serenade* (to Tchaikovsky's Serenade for Strings), moods are indicated; in *Scotch Symphony* (Mendelssohn), there is almost a plot; in *Square Dance*, he related music of Vivaldi and Corelli with square dance calls and formations.

Stravinsky never intended his Concerto Grosso in D to be a ballet, yet it is versatile enough to serve as a brilliant and powerful base for Robbins's *The Cage*. Mahler's *Kindertotenlieder* is a song cycle, but it has become a ballet companion through Tudor's *Dark Elegies* just as a later song cycle, Britten's *Illuminations,* found an even more vivid resolution in Ashton's ballet of the tortured, decadent poet Rimbaud.

It should also be made clear that there is more than one way to interpret, choreographically, the same piece of music. There is more than one version of Prokofieff's *Romeo and Juliet* or Orff's *Carmina Burana* or Stravinsky's *Danses Concertantes*. Certainly, nothing could be further apart than the late Doris Humphrey's modern dance setting of the Bach Passacaglia and Fugue in C Minor and Roland Petit's *Le Jeune Homme et la Mort* (with book by Cocteau). In the former, Humphrey sought to translate into formal movement the grandeur, the nobility, of the music as well as to mirror its phrasings, its sonorities, its rhythms. Petit used the Bach score as an ironic commentary on the sordid passions which moved on it and over it. Both were valid theater uses of Bach.

In its incipiency, ballet used music that dance itself, the popular dances of the day, had inspired. Today is little different, for our own folk rhythms, country style or city jazz, have found their way into ballet scores. Morton Gould, for one, has let the jazz idiom speak through him for contemporary ballet scores, just as Copland has harkened to the barn, the village green, the prairie and the range for airs and rhythms suitable to the needs of his choreographers.

Dance and music, then, have always fed each other. True, there have been periods of disdainful fasting, and both arts suffered. But from the days of the passepieds to today's way-out beats and rhythms, the choreographer and the composer have challenged each other, infuriated each other and, very often, inspired the best from each other. Ted Shawn, dance innovator, once described music and dance as being "twin shoots from the same bulb." The centuries-old art of ballet has long made manifest his theory—dance and music are separate but, in the last analysis, inseparable.

Chapter 4

The Designer

The decorative aspect of ballet—the settings and the costumes—varies in importance from maximal to minimal. Historically, design is the fourth basic ingredient of ballet, following dance, music and libretto (or book or theme). And, at the start of it all, design was the major element, for in the great banquet fêtes of the fourteenth and fifteenth centuries in Italy, ballet technique had not even evolved from the simple court dances of the day. Spectacle, then, was an essential for those aristocratic galas which celebrated a marriage, honored a prince or stood as a testament to the power and wealth of an ambitious aristocrat.

At the other end of the ballet spectrum is undecorated dancing, spare and pure. For our age, Balanchine has stated this brilliantly in any of a number of ballets, "music visualizations," which require no setting and no costumes other than simple, unadorned, black-and-white classroom apparel. His enormously successful *Concerto Barocco* originally had elaborate costumes and setting by Eugene Berman, one of the major designers for ballet in the twentieth century. Ultimately, Balanchine discarded the Berman designs. They obscured *his,* Balanchine's, choreographic designs. It was the purity of action which was to be paramount.

Balanchine is not indulging in an idiosyncrasy when he determines that one of his creations shall be done without scenery and without costumes other than classroom-type uniforms. In modern dance, when Martha Graham broke away from the ethnic materials which constituted the core of the Denishawn Company, she directed herself to an exploration and exploitation of the body and its movement potentials. She and her dancers generally wore stark, form-fitting, skirted (to the floor) dresses which covered the frame not with decor but with bland modesty. Graham herself refers to this as "the period of long woolens."

Yet St. Denis never looked upon her often elaborate draperies as body decor—"I use them as extensions of the movements of the human body into space."

But in the early days of ballet, decor of the most elaborate sort was there not simply to set the scene or to indicate a period or place, but for its own sake as sheer spectacle.

Le Ballet Comique de la Reine, for example, made use of what was known as *décor simultané,* that is, multiple settings. In the great hall in which the *Ballet Comique* was presented nearly four hundred years ago, the audience sat in galleries on two sides, the royal family sat at one end of the hall, and at the other end and along the sides were the settings which included the grove of Pan, a bank of clouds, a grotto with flowers and beasts and, in the distance, Circe's palace. Jacques Patin was the designer of this lavish multi-setting and of the opulent costumes which went with it.

The depth of the performing areas in the great palace halls, or sometimes out-of-doors in vast courtyards, invited a concept of scenery which was to evolve for the theater itself. Thus, when ballet spectacle moved onto a true stage, depth was retained in fact or in illusion. Some of the Italian spectacles, for example, took place on three planes: on the floor of the hall itself, on an elevated stage with a big apron curving outward, and in air on cloud machines! The artist's command of perspective was exploited even more fully, when the spectacle was no longer presented in a hall where the floor could be used or where a deep apron was feasible. Here, the scenery provided the illusion of long vistas almost without end, be they colonnaded walks, enormous grottoes, streets reaching toward a distant city or castle, skies and seas seemingly extending toward infinity.

This "depth" concept of stage scenery as it was employed in the seventeenth and eighteenth centuries may still be seen first-hand at the marvelously preserved Court Theater at Drottningholm, the one-time summer residence of Sweden's kings, not far, by today's travel standards, from Stockholm. Most of Europe's court theaters burned up (a common theatrical hazard before the era of electric lights), were torn down or were modernized. Drottningholm's preservation was due to a fluke of fate. When the old theater became obsolete and when the Royal Court moved elsewhere for its summer seasons and when bigger and grander opera houses were built, Drottningholm's theater was not destroyed. No one bothered to get rid of it. It was simply used as a granary for the royal livestock. The scenery, the spectacle effects (such as rolling waves and ascending-descending clouds), even a curtain dating back to the days of Queen Christina, and the elaborate networks of ropes which controlled the spectacle effects were either pushed to one side or covered up with grain. So it was that when a theater historian began probing Sweden's great dance and opera heritage, he came upon the miraculously preserved Court Theater and all its trappings at Drottningholm.

Today, Drottningholm plays a major role in Sweden's festivals of music and ballet. Here you may sit on seats each clearly reserved for members of the royal entourage, and you may even sit in a latticed box where a king's unofficial favorite observed the performance. The royal box itself is, of course, still reserved for His Majesty. And as the curtain rises on a re-creation of an old ballet or upon a Gluck opera, your eyes will travel down the deep, almost endless vistas familiar to spectacle-goers of centuries ago. The stage itself is unusually narrow—court theaters are not very big, since they were made only for the pleasure of a monarch and his invited guests—but it is surprisingly deep, not only in perspective but in fact. It has to be, by the old standards.

Suppose there is a sea scene. To create an illusion of the sea, Drottningholm has at its disposal six enormous wooden rollers, rather like giant rolling pins. They are splashed with blue and white paint, for the sea and the breakers, and it takes twelve men, six on either side of the stage, to crank them into turbulent, beautiful action. At Drottningholm, the ancient spectacle survives.

It also survives in more modern opera houses. In Copenhagen, the Danes also have their old court theater, and although it is mainly used as a museum, special performances take place on its narrow but deep and steeply raked (or sloped) stage. But in the much, much newer Royal Theater,

the official home of Denmark's ballet, opera and drama, stage
depth is retained to the degree that in a ballet such as *Napoli*
the Blue Grotto of Capri can be effectively reproduced with
room enough for a boat, a boatman and some genuine choreographic navigation.

If, today, we have barely equaled in imagination the spectacular scenic effects achieved in the days of Catherine de
Medici and Louis XIV, in the masques of Ben Jonson, in the
lovely little miracles of the court theater, we have also hardly
touched the costume potential that our ancestors created for
ballet. True, in our own century, we have seen ballets with
scenery and costumes by such avant-garde artists as Salvador
Dali, but three centuries ago, designers made up extravagant
costumes ranging from fanciful reproductions of musical instruments through dress and appurtenances identifying the
shoemaker, the silversmith (bellows and all) and the architect to wildly surrealist suggestions of hermaphrodites.

Louis himself, the Sun King, was dazzlingly costumed for
his role of Apollo. But if the King wore gorgeous trappings
for his participation in various court ballets, his horses were
even more spectacular, and horse-ballets were enormously
popular. Not only were the choreographic formations striking when performed by a corps of horses, but the trappings,
such as in *La Carrousel de Louis XIV*, were both fanciful
and resplendent.

In this horse-ballet, for example, one of the characters on
horseback was the "King of the Americans," and since he was
supposed to represent a savage chieftain, his mount was
equally awesome. The saddlecloth was a sort of tigerskin
bordered with gold, but the tail and the mane had been
transformed into masses of writhing, tongue-darting snakes,

and, of course, a horn from the forehead suggested a magical unicorn. Henri Gissey, a highly imaginative artist, designed costumes not only for humans but also for the dancing horses.

Of the many fine designers of the Louis XIV period, Jean Berain was one of the most distinguished. His costumes in the rich, classical court style were both opulent and elegant, and those which were planned to symbolize various trades and occupations—architect, musician, smith—were fantastic and usually amusing.

Court convention in dress did not allow for anything remotely resembling ethnic or period authenticity. The dancing ladies wore costumes (hooped) which nearly reached the floor, and the gentlemen frequently wore dress which included a skirtlike affair, also hooped, which reached to just above the knee. So it was that a Faun's costume had no suggestion of ancient Greece about it—the skirt, garters at the knee, plumed headdress, were all there. Neptune would be similarly dressed, with only a trident suggesting his identity. Apollo, with a laurel wreath and a lyre, was dressed like a seventeenth-century courtier or king. A village lass was dressed as richly as a princess, you might guess at a Chinese because his hat faintly suggested a pagoda, but an African was costumed as if he lived along the Seine rather than the Niger.

The same conventional elegance of dress would be found, say, for a Fury or a Demon, only a dagger in hand or images of snakes and frightening heads appliquéd on the hooped skirts of both male and female would lead the viewer to expect that evil was afoot.

Fashions in dress at court became even more extravagant. Great panniers swept out, ellipitcally, from a tiny waist, to cover enormous expanses of territory. Louis Bouquet, the designer, has recorded these extravagances in costumes which make one think of a ball rather than a ballet.

Camargo, of course, rebelled against such dress. And, as we know, she shortened the skirts, took off the high heels of her shoes and did away with impossible ellipses of skirting so that she could dance, just as her colleague, Sallé, discarded panniers and armadas as head pieces. Still and all the costumes clung to the playfulness of the court to the degree that a farmerette was dressed like a countess and only a delicate sickle in her hand identified her with agricultural labors.

With the French Revolution, all changed, on stage as well as off. The costumes became far less cumbersome, sometimes even achieving the simplicity of classical Greek or Roman tunics and draperies. Costumes for characters from exotic lands strove for a new authenticity so that an East Indian girl would wear a dress simulating a sari, with the short-sleeved vest and trousers and the long braid of hair.

The ballerinas continued to wear the Camargo-length skirt (slightly shorter) but the hoops, panniers and ellipses were gone forever. True, the skirts were generally circular but light and bouffant—they floated and danced with the body rather than imprisoning it. The early 1800's gave us the prelude to the Romantic Age of ballet, heralding the coming of the historic *La Sylphide*, with costumes by Eugene Lami.

Marie Taglioni's costume as the Sylphide was all gauze and froth, as ethereal, as airy, as evanescent as the fairy creature herself who flitted through the woods, above the branches, up chimneys, through casement windows. Here was the embodiment of the female at her purest, her most spiritual, always desirable, ever unattainable. The costume for this new age of ballet, for the new vision of woman, was as important as the recently introduced dancing on pointe which elevated the female to a new plane, above mere man. *La Sylphide* in practice clothes? Impossible!

It is very likely that Taglioni herself (who had worn somewhat similar dress in the long-popular *Flore et Zéphire*) and her choreographer father had something to say about the costume for the Sylphide and, indeed, about the settings, but it was Lami who designed them, and his costume for the ballerina became standard (no matter what the colors or decorations) for every classical-romantic ballerina to come, right down to this day.

Not only were the national costumes much closer to true ethnic sources than were those fanciful creations under the Louis kings, but when peasants were to be indicated, the dress adhered much more closely to rustic styles. The performers were dancers playing at being peasants rather than aristocrats pretending that brocades and plumes were the usual adornment of the common villager.

Indians, Spaniards, Tyroleans, Gypsies became identifiable. Theater, of course, required certain adaptations and dance even more, but the intent was now perfectly clear.

With the rising of the ballerina onto her personal pedestal of the pointe, with the new adulation of the female, came the bubblings of women's emancipation. On the ballet stage, there were harem revolts, lady brigands, amazons and other militant sisters. In no time at all, military ladies in battle formations became high points of ballets and their music hall counterparts. Long before Annie Oakley, the gun-toting lass was a favorite in the theater of dance, and her popularity, particuarly en masse, was to last throughout the century.

The surrealist, pop-art, fantasy-founded costumes were no more limited to the seventeenth and eighteenth centuries than they are exclusive to today. Ballet, in the 1800's, turned up not simply with pussycats and wolves and mice but also with costumes which suggested enormous cabbages or, perhaps, a leafy figure with a radish head. There would also be birds and butterflies and, naturally, flowers of every hue and shape. Even a century later, Louella Gear, the comedienne, was to lament: "I'm a Paramount-Publix-Roxy Rose. . . . I've been a pansy for Pantages, a cactus for Balaban-Katz . . . but I want to be myself, a personality, not a lousy rose."

With the change of classical ballet dress in the nineteenth century, came a change in decor. It wasn't that it was less grandiose but, rather, that it was more mystical, suiting the new themes of the Romantic Age. *La Sylphide* had its vast baronial hall but it also had its Scottish woodland, misty and mysterious, just as the immortal *Giselle* moved from peasant cottage and rural clearing to ensorcelled woods peopled by creatures of doom. *La Péri* from Persia or *Ondine* from the sea required as elaborate settings as the court ballets once demanded, only the accent changed to give substance to poetry, to evoke fantasy.

With the passing of the Romantic Age (its masterpieces, such as *Giselle,* of course, endured) and the coming of Marius Petipa in Imperial Russia, designs for the ballet underwent further changes. The ballerina's skirt, her tutu, crept upward to reveal her knees. It wasn't a very pretty line, but it served a new fashion in movement. Camargo had docked her skirt so that her public could see her mastery of the entrechat. The Petipa ballerina shortened hers even further so that her admirers could truly see the miracle of thirty-two fouettés and other new phenomena of dancing limbs.

Still, certain charming idiocies of costume continued. The now-shortened tutu, a bell-like affair around the thighs, was almost inescapable. If the ballerina were a peasant, an apron over the tutu would do the trick; Spanish, a shawl; a bacchante, some grapes. But it really didn't matter, for the steps were always those, for the ballerina and danseur, of the classical dance no matter what the role. In the national dance divertissements in, say, *Swan Lake* or *The Sleeping Beauty*, a pretty good stab was made at getting somewhere close to ethnic verity in step and dress, but not for the romantic leads.

And it was in this area that young Michel Fokine rebelled, at the turn of the century, against the age of Petipa from which he had sprung. Fokine's Egyptians (*Cléopâtre*) would wear at least simulated Pharoahnic dress, his Greeks would be clad in tunics echoing the designs on ancient sculptures and frescoes, his Orientals would wear the exotica of their homelands and his Russians would look Russian. His revolt, of course, was against the old-style movement which served any situation, for his chief concern was with the extending of the vistas of choreography. But along with his search and research for movements suitable and changing with each different subject, came the necessity of a new approach to theater dress.

With the coming of Diaghileff and the great Ballets Russes, the Fokine rebellion burst out of Russia itself and jolted the complacent, weary and almost dead ballet of western Europe with a series of breathtaking performances in Paris and other capitals. The choreography was new but so also were the designs for scenery and costumes, designs which represented the enormous talents of not only the great theatrical artists of the day but also the world's greatest painters, who were themselves rebels, innovators, explorers.

Beginning with Russia's Bakst (*Spectre de la Rose, Carnaval, Scheherazade,* the costumes for *Firebird* and other ballets) and Benois (*Les Sylphides, Petrouchka,* the Russian re-creation of *Giselle*), the ballet scene moved on to a fabulous array of designers of all nationalities.

From 1909 to the death of Diaghileff in 1929, a fantastic array of painters served the ballet. Nicholas Roerich designed both *Prince Igor* (the dance suite), which turned Paris topsy-turvy, and the later *Sacre du Printemps,* which had Parisians booing, hissing and raging. Natalia Gontcharova dazzled the eye with her sun-burst colors in *Coq d'Or.* Pablo Picasso, the great cubist, designed *Parade* and *Pulcinella,* and our own Robert Edmond Jones made the fantastic setting for Nijinsky's *Tyl Eulenspiegel.*

Picasso also designed the highly successful *Tricorne,* and other great painters who poured their talents into the Diaghileff repertory were José Maria Sert, Michel Larionov, Fernand Léger, Marie Laurencin.

Diaghileff was not the only one served by a variety of great painters and great designers. André Dérain, Giorgio di Chirico, Bérard, Dufy, Tchelitchev, Berman, Chappell, Stevenson, John Piper, Matisse, Dali and others lent their talents to ballet.

For Massine's *Rouge et Noir,* Matisse actually painted his patterns on the foot-to-neck tights which the dancers wore. He was concerned with the contours of each body and painted his abstract designs to be in harmony with the shape of each body. Thus, someone like Alicia Markova became a living easel for one of the great painters of the age.

Dali brought to the stage his wild surrealist dreams for *Bacchanale, Labyrinth* and others, where the dancers could move in and around and through huge swans or human torsos with avenues running through them, limp clocks, popping umbrellas and other Dali delights.

Not all designers of major theater presentations have been easel artists. England's Cecil Beaton and America's Oliver Smith, although they may sketch and draw and paint, are famous for what they bring to the stage.

Smith, who has designed innumerable Broadway shows as well as ballets, works in many styles, depending on the theme of a ballet or the needs of a given choreographer. His marvelously mobile settings for Agnes de Mille's *Fall River Legend* range from the literal New England parlor of the 1890's to a melodramatic backdrop in which the same scene is reproduced in bloody fantasy. His basic setting, which is architectural, is swiftly transformed from a house to a church to a gallows.

The stature of a designer for ballet should not be underestimated, even though the days of kingly largesse are gone and the cost of onstage castles, lakes, clouds, flying (by wires) performers, grottoes, belching volcanos, ships heaving at sea on stormy waves is almost (not always) prohibitive. In 1944, Oliver Smith was one of the triumvirate who made American ballet history—it was he who designed *Fancy Free*, the ballet that catapulted Jerome Robbins to choreographic fame and Leonard Bernstein to new musical renown. Twenty-one years later, Smith and Robbins were reunited (there were many collaborations in between) for another masterpiece, Stravinsky's *Les Noces*, also produced by the American Ballet Theatre. The Smith setting for *Fancy Free* was any and all bars in New York City planted somewhere below the majestic skyline. The Smith setting for *Les Noces* was dominated by gigantic paintings of dour saints looking down, seemingly as they had done for ages unestimated, upon mere man.

These ancient images served Robbins superbly, for against them he placed a boy and a girl who found each other, not because of, but in spite of an ageless ritual which had united them under faded but fearsome ancestral eyes.

Marc Chagall, the painter, and Rouben Ter-Arutunian, designer, serve the art of dancing with equal brilliance. The art of ballet is honored by a Rouault (*Prodigal Son*), but it can also get along without the collaboration of painters and designers, for a comparatively new art of theater production has brought new visual magic to the stage. It is the art of lighting. Stages have been lit, of course, by one method or another for hundreds of years. Early in this century, Loie Fuller experimented with the miracle of light and made light a major ingredient in her dances of moths and butterflies and flames and flowers. Ruth St. Denis was as concerned with lighting effects as she was with decor and dress. A new age was introduced in which lighting did not simply illuminate the stage; it transformed it.

The New York City Ballet was the first major company to depend more on lighting effects than upon elaborate decor and costumes. This was partly a matter of economic necessity, for in the late 1940's and 1950's, the young company had not received its millions from the Ford Foundation, yet its

director, George Balanchine, was enormously prolific. Balanchine charged little or nothing at all for his ballets, but
mounting them was quite another matter, and funds were
strictly limited.

So along came a number of ballets with simple or no settings at all and with dancers wearing classroom dress or very
modest costumes. It was up the to the sorceress of stage lighting, Jean Rosenthal, to make the public as fulfilled with lighting effects as, in the posh days of ballet, they had been with
Bakst or Picasso or Dali. This is not to say that in its first
decade the New York City Ballet had no real productions. It
had some beautiful ones with stunning scenery and costumes,
but it also had a host of ballets which were composed only of
dancing, music and lighting. *Serenade, Concerto Barocco,
Sylvia Pas de Deux, Allegro Brillante, Minkus Pas de Trois,
Glinka Pas de Trois* and many more needed only the lumi-
nous dress provided by Miss Rosenthal.

Even in a dramatic ballet such as Jerome Robbins's *The
Cage,* Miss Rosenthal whipped up some eerie decor with
spider-like ropes, all of which cost less than two dollars for
materials, but added to it pools and pathways and pinpoints,
shafts and slices of light which gave brilliant disclosure to
this macabre and terrifying ballet.

Although lighting can replace costumes and scenery with
great effectiveness—indeed, certain ballets are better off with
no decoration other than that supplied by lighting—it can
also serve settings and props and costumes brilliantly. A Jean
Rosenthal or a Thomas Skelton or any of their colleagues
would light a flat drop differently from a sculptured piece or
a vista differently from an intimate scene.

The colors, intensities and directions of their lights (from the footlights, from above, from the sides, from spots) would be governed not simply by place but by character. Who is being lighted? What is the situation? What is the mood? What, in fact, is the rhythm of the piece?

Lighting for the ballet not only defines figures, it discloses intent. It can omen and augur as surely as a Greek chorus of voices, and it can probe mercilessly. Its potential ranges from the command of the beautiful female dance star who said to her lighting crew, "Just make me look pretty," to the blazing lights of Balanchine's *Opus 34* which seemed to strip skin off bodies to reveal the red rush of nervous systems and, at the close, to turn upon the audience with searing, clinical, blinding rays.

Related to both decor and lighting are the screen projections which the modern dancers, especially the avant-garde group, and the ballet itself use on occasion. Here are magic lantern slides, a sort of record of life itself (as distinct from created designs), juxtaposed with the immediate living on-stage. Movies, as well as stills, are effective in giving a setting an atmosphere, realistic, romantic or fantastic, to the theater of dance. What better way to suggest flames than through moving, lighted projections upon a background? Or can flames be better suggested by the flashing red capes of the Spanish dancers in Act III of *Swan Lake* as they frame the thirty-two fouettés of the evil Odile in the production done by the Ballet of the Stanislavsky Theater?

Is one method better than another? You decide. There is nothing quite like Cloud Nine descending from the skies to make special magic in a restoration of a spectacular court ballet. And there is nothing quite like a rosy light to illumine the magic of a Fonteyn, a Tallchief, a Plisetskaya, a Suzanne Farrell as she makes public her special and very own dance intimacies.

Chapter 5

Ballet Dress

The designer for ballet, no matter what his fancies may be for the adornment of the body, ninety-nine percent of the time must work with, or around, a traditional and basic piece of dance dress, tights. This is literally a skin-tight garment which covers the body from the waist down. It is of one piece and, customarily, it covers the feet as well as the legs. If bare feet are required, as they are in modern dance and in some modern ballets, the tights will end at the ankle. But for classical ballet, the feet are encased by the tights and over them go the toe shoe for the female dancer, the soft ballet shoe for the man or, if required, character shoes, such as boots.

Tights may be made of various materials. For rehearsals and classes, especially in winter, wool is preferred simply because it keeps the legs warm, and warm legs are limber legs, less prone to accident than cold legs. But for the stage, the silken look is required. Until the invention of nylon and its family of related fabrics, silk stockings were preferred above all. Tights, of course, must stretch, but they must also remain tight, for if there are wrinkles at the knee (especially), the ankle, in the seat or at the crotch, tights no longer do what they are intended to do and that is to preserve exactly the contours of the body.

With today's miracle fabrics, tights are made which permit, say, kneebends but which will sheathe the leg without wrinkle when it is straightened.

The female dancer secures the tights in single thickness right at the waistline. Over them she may wear a tutu (romantic-classical length to the calf; very short, like a large

Tights

powder puff around the hips) or a leotard or a tunic or some other type costumes.

The male dancer, on the other hand, can wear his tights in two different ways. If he is going to wear a vest, tunic, jacket or coat, he will pull the upper section of the tights slightly over the ribcage of the body and keep them in place by suspenders over the shoulders (the suspenders, of course, are concealed by the outer costume). However, he may wish to wear only a T-shirt for class or a noncostumed ballet, and for this, he will pull the tights as high as they will go (partly over the ribs), take a narrow black belt and pull it tightly around the waist and then roll the excess tights material above the waist around the belt. This keeps the tights tight and defines the waistline neatly with the material of the tights itself secured and outlined by a concealed belt.

Tights? Where did they come from? Their origins may well go back to Camargo in the early years of the eighteenth century. The great ballerina, as we know, in the days long before toe shoes and tutus, wanted to be an aerial dancer, a virtuoso like the male. As the first female to master the entrechat, not only did she cut off her floor-length skirt to the calf and remove the heels of her slippers so that she could get a good spring into the air, but she also found it advisable to invent something called *caleçon de précaution*, or emergency drawers. The story is that a colleague of Camargo's, who had also shortened her skirt and taken to the air, caught her dress on a bit of scenery in the midst of a jump so that her body was bared to the point of embarrassment. Actually, she fainted. Camargo realized that such an accident could happen to anyone. Hence the *caleçon de précaution*, which eventually developed into tights.

The male dancer need not wear anything over the tights, although in certain period costumes he may wear balloon-like knickers of Elizabethan cut or short-short pants (such as the peasants wear in certain productions of *La Fille Mal Gardée*, or as the Soviet dancers wore as standard attire on their first visits to America) or a tunic or doublet which comes down close to the hip line.

But the male dancer *must* wear an article of apparel under his tights. Sometimes this resembles any form-fitting, stretchable underpants, such as jockey shorts. Soviet male dancers usually wear these as do some American modern dancers. Usually, however, the male ballet dancers wear a dance belt. This is made of strong cloth and wide elastic. The unstretchable cloth part is something like a panel which goes, loincloth fashion, from the abdominal area, between the legs (where it narrows) and up to the waist in back. At the sides and across the back is the elastic part of the belt.

Some boys, when they are just starting ballet training, don't know how to wear a dance belt, any more than they know how to secure tights neatly. The instinct is to put on

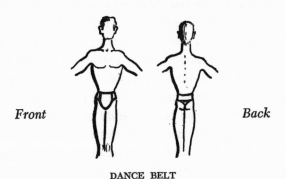

Front *Back*

DANCE BELT

the dance belt with the broadest part of the non-elastic material in back. This is all wrong, for wearing it this way cuts the cheeks of the buttocks at an unbecoming angle. The narrowest part of the nonelastic material is worn in back and is pulled tightly between the cheeks of the buttocks so as not to distort in any way the contour of that part of the body. The wide, nonelastic part is worn in front and provides support not merely for the abdomen but chiefly for the male genitals. In wearing a dance belt, the male organ is almost always positioned upward against the abdomen—this is called, among athletes and dancers, to "dress up."

The female dancer may also wear a version of the dance belt. This, of course, would be of different cut and would be solely for abdominal support. Most female dancers prefer not to wear one, believing that muscle strength (or a muscle-girdle) is nature's best way for keeping the abdomen flat. Dancers who have had babies, however, are likely to wear them. In most instances, the female dancer wears under her tights very brief pants, "exactly like bikinis," as the ballerina Toni Lander describes them.

Over her tights, the female dancer frequently wears a tutu. This is a skirt made of multiple layers of light cloth, which, however, will hold its shape. Tarlatan is the traditional material for the tutu, although other materials can be used, including silk or nylon-family fabrics. The tutu can and does vary in length. For the romantic era of ballet, symbolized by Marie Taglioni and the *La Sylphide* of 1832, the tutu may reach from any point just below the calf to the ankle. The tutu for classical style may start just above the knee or be so brief that it simply frames the hips. Giselle, in Act II, wears a tutu that is ankle-length; Princess Aurora in *The Sleeping Beauty* wears a powder-puff style tutu.

The tutu of romantic length floats and billows and wafts with the gentlest of movements, thus giving a misty as well as mystic quality to the half-real, half-fanciful heroines of the romantic ballets.

The short tutus reveal the entire leg and are perfect for displays of virtuosity, such as the thirty-two fouettés in Act III of *Swan Lake*. The basic tutu is made of tarlatan pants on top of which are sewn several graded rows of tarlatan frills. Atop this explosion of frills can be a silk or velvet cover, jeweled or designed, and of any color the ballet requires.

The tutu is sewn to a tight, tapered bodice so that the costume, other than the tights which go under the tutu, is of one piece.

For classroom exercise or for modern abstract ballets, the tutu is unnecessary and in its place the dancer wears a leotard. This may best be described as a one-piece bathing suit. It is usually sleeveless but not necessarily. It is worn over the tights and the underpants, although some dancers, when wearing leotards, find that underpants are not needed. Practice leotards are usually black, but they can be white or, indeed, of any color, depending on what the designer or the choreographer may wish. In a ballet such as Jerome Robbins's *The Cage*, the basic costume is a leotard, but one which uses appliqué patterns pertinent to a work in which the dancers are insect-like creatures.

Tights may also be of any color, but customarily the female dancer wears pink tights with any costume—although for an exotic role, they might be all-blue, all-purple, all-red (with toe shoes to match), and the male dancer wears white, black or, perhaps, grey. The danseur is more likely to wear tights and slippers of different colors than is the ballerina, for whom pink tights and pink toe shoes are the most becoming.

Toe shoes, of course, are a comparatively recent addition to ballet. It is too easy and it is also inaccurate to think of toe dancing and ballet as synonymous.

Ballet existed, grew and developed in virtuosity for more than two hundred years before dancing "sur les pointes" became a part of the movement vocabulary of ballet. The evolution was slow and sensible. Camargo shed the heels of her shoes in order to get a better spring, but she did not dance on pointe, and neither did her immediate successors. With

Camargo, in the early 1700's, the ballerina had made great advances: the shortened skirt, the heel-less slipper, the entre-chat, the incipient tights, flight as well as fleetness. She had mastered the ninety-degree turnout of the limbs, allowing for instant command of direction forward, backward, side-ways, diagonals. And it is certain that she disciplined her foot to point sharply and cleanly. This very act of pointing the toe to the degree that there is no break at the ankle and the foot becomes, literally, a smooth extension of the leg it-self, has caused dance historians no end of problems. Critics of the 1700's referred to "beautiful" or "fantastic" toes. What did they mean? That the ballerina stood on toe, tip-toe and not half-toe, or that the stretch of the foot was remarkable?

In some instances of such reporting, we shall never know what transpired. But it is certain that dancing on toe took place long before Taglioni's *La Sylphide* of 1832. Almost half a century before the historic *La Sylphide,* which made the pointe an essential to ballet, the female dancer had bal-lanced, briefly and precariously, on pointe. She had no blocked, boxed, supported toe shoes. She simply had strong feet, and she rose onto pointe, or stepped onto pointe, for a suspenseful instant.

It is very likely that the first, or one of the first, ballerinas to dance on pointe did so about 1790, for a Mlle. Millerd was said to have a "fantastic toe" and she danced in a ballet, *Flore et Zéphire,* which was danced by Taglioni at a much later date. So if Taglioni made dancing on the toe a prerequi-site of ballet performing in 1832, it is equally certain that she and a generation of her predecessors did exactly the same thing in the near-half-century of dancing which took place before that historic date.

The slippers worn by Taglioni and her rival ballerinas were very soft. Alicia Markova, who owns a pair of Taglioni shoes, says, "They are as soft as kid gloves." The only support for the foot comes from some modest darning along the sides and under, not directly beneath, the toes themselves. To this day, professional dancers will tell you that it isn't what you actually stand on—the toe or toes—which requires protection

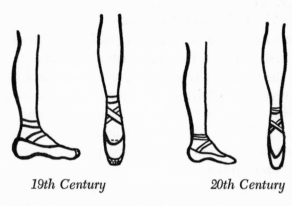

19th Century   20th Century

POINTE SLIPPERS

but, rather, the sides where the toes must not sprawl but become a single dancing unit.

With such limited support for the foot, the ballerina of the late 1700's and early 1800's could not begin to do the virtuosic pointe work which is merely routine for today's dancer. There were no pirouettes on pointe, no piqué turns, no fouettés, no yards of bourrées across the stage, no hops on pointe. The ballerina stepped, stood or rose for an awesome moment on her "fantastic toe."

Today, the ballerina's foot is not handled with kid gloves. It is encased. The evolution had taken place gradually—extra darning, extra thickness, extra protections of all kinds. The toe shoe today is almost a contraption. The sides and the actual pointe are made of cloth covered with satin. Along the top is a drawstring which holds the shoe fast to the foot. Underneath the pointe itself there are seven layers of cloth held together by special glues. Thus, there are seven fabrics, of varying thicknesses, between the bare toe and the floor of the stage. A leather sole, shorter and narrower than the foot itself, provides still further support.

The novice, or the pupil who is put into toe shoes before she has had the proper training, needs all the support she can get, for she is not really a dancer, just an amateur trickster. So it is very easy for this unfortunate beginner to obtain toe shoes with a thick, unyielding box for a pointe and with an inflexible sole. It is almost impossible to dance with such fetters on the foot, but the beginner, poorly trained, can at least get up onto tippy-toes and stagger about for the pleasure of her relatives at the annual school recital. But this is neither ballet nor dancing; it is simply a misapplied trick.

The ballerina or, indeed, the properly trained young professional in a corps de ballet knows how to use her feet. She can stand on full pointe in soft ballet slippers (not toe shoes), and some can stand barefoot on toe. Naturally, she cannot spin or hop this way, but she has not bought a many-layered contrivance to take the place of discipline. She needs a toe shoe for multiple turns and other virtuosities, but the strength to accomplish them is already in her control of her body (yes, dancing on toe is as much in the body, perhaps more, as it is in the feet themselves).

The professional female dancer in ballet doesn't want her foot to be imprisoned. She wants to feel the floor through the pointe. She wants the sole to be flexible so she can move her foot as if it were unshod. In a word, she wants to control her foot, instead of having the inanimate shoe govern it.

Most ballerinas, therefore, like a soft toe shoe. They order malleable soles. They beat the pointe against the floor manually to soften the box. Some even put the pointe of a new toe shoe in a door frame and slam the door on it to break it, to soften it.

For lyrical ballets, ballerinas wear old, soft toe shoes, so that the jump has greater spring and the landing a softer conclusion. Thirty-two fouettés? New shoes (at least for the left foot) are a must, because it is possible, on certain stages, to go right through seven layers of fabric before the tour to force is completed. But let's use that battered toe shoe for the gentle *Les Sylphides* tomorrow night.

The point to remember, if you are a young dancer, is that the toe shoe is merely an aid. Ballet existed long before the "box" came into being, and ballet today lives because of the miracle of the foot, not because of cloth and glue, satin and threads.

The foot is an extremity of the body. What about the other end, the head? The ballerina is required to wear everything from invisible hairsprays to feathers and hats and crowns.

"I just don't know what we girls did before hairspray was invented," says the Danish-born ballerina Toni Lander. Before Miss Lander's generation came along, hairnets provided the answer, for a ballerina could not permit her hair to fall in disarray if she did a pirouette or plummeted toward the floor in the "fish" step.

Along with hairnets and hairsprays go hairpins, an abundance of hairpins. "I don't know how many pins she uses

when she has to wear a little crown," says Donald Coleman,
Melissa Hayden's husband, "but I do know that when I'm
waiting to take her home after a performance, it seems to
take her forever to get those damn pins out."

Coronets on the very top of the head—they don't fit over
the brow like a proper crown—constitute a trademark for the
classical ballerina when she is dancing regal roles. Since she
is almost always a princess, this is an indication of rank as
well as being a symbol of radiant loveliness.

Wreath   Coronet   Tiara

The ballerina of the Romantic Age of ballet wore wreaths
instead of miniature crowns, but these too required pins. After all, a rakish wreath would be unbecoming to a distant,
delicate, virginal creature.

Today's ballerina uses pins for her crown, her wreath, for
a spray of jewels or flowers or for whatever she must wear
on her head. Pins, enough of them, will do the job, along
with hairspray or nets. But some dancers use concealed rib-
bons. Miss Lander, for example, uses a narrow velvet ribbon
under her hair. It goes from the back of the neck to the top

of the head and with the velvet side turned down toward the roots of the hair; this keeps it from skidding. Then the long hair, or a switch, is pulled over it and the hairpins (usually bobbypins) then secure the coronet to the hidden velvet ribbon.

The ballerina is so accustomed to her crown that she feels almost undressed without it or an equivalent headpiece. Maria Tallchief, the great ballerina of American Indian blood, was once honored by her own people, the Osages, who made her a princess of the tribe. Tallchief was deeply moved by the occasion, for she is proud of her heritage, but she confessed later, "I really do feel more comfortable in a ballet crown than in feathers!"

Sometimes, the dancer (both male and female) must wear wigs. In modern times, of course, quick hair-dyes which can be washed out immediately after a performance (or between scenes in a ballet!) can transform a blond into a black-haired Spanish dancer or, perhaps, into a dark Saracen or a jet-haired Oriental. But often a period style hairdo is needed, or it may be that uniformity is essential to the choreographic concept of an ensemble scene, so wigs are in order.

Wigs are made to be close-fitting, but with the strenuous movement required of dancers, no chances can be taken that the hairpiece will sail out into the orchestra pit or slip over one eye. Wigs, then, usually have a fringe of nylon net which extends beyond the natural hairline and which can be glued (with spirit gum) to the skin itself. A touch of makeup over the net, and the audience cannot see it at all. For top security measures, the ballerina might also add her tightly drawn hair-ribbon and use pins to secure the wig to her own hair. This means that ribbon, pins, nylon net and glue are part of the impedimenta necessary to keep on wigs and crowns and head decors.

The hair-ribbon, as an adjunct to makeup for the theater, should not be underestimated. In addition to its services to crowns and wigs, it can accomplish other fine effects. Ruth St. Denis, the great American dance pioneer, cast many of her dance masterpieces in Oriental mold. Under a jet wig, she would wear a narrow, ribbon-like tape which she pulled so tightly that it lifted the contours of the face itself into an Oriental cast. She found this to give a far more authentic look to an Eastern character than simply painting slanted eyelines on a Western face. It often gave her a headache, so tight was the knot, but it worked. Once, when a middle-aged dancer came to Miss St. Denis for advice on Oriental makeup and was instructed on the proper use of the hidden tape, the veteran performer scrutinized her visitor and said, as only one female can say to another, "Aside from the Oriental look, my dear, in about five years you're going to need that tape anyway!"

Chapter 6

Ballet Training

Where to study ballet? In America, that is the big question. There are thousands of private dance schools, and they range from excellent ballet academies with fine faculties and expertly graded courses to classes held in a makeshift studio —a basement with cement floors and poor ventilation—under the guidance of a teacher who may be incompetent or so ignorant of the body and its proper training that the child's well-being could actually be imperiled.

In other lands, it is much easier to know where to find the best ballet instruction. State theaters, incorporating their ballet companies and ballet schools, are quite likely to provide the best instruction available, although there are teachers of genius in many countries who work outside of royal and state theaters.

The European method, in the royal or national theaters, is to combine academic education with dance education. This, in most respects, is the ideal system, for it provides homogeneity of training and exposure to art and learning. Such an academy will have a style, perhaps even a stamp, which makes it distinctive. Furthermore, many of its ballet pupils will progress from classroom to stage within the same theater complex. Is it small wonder, then, that the dancers of the Royal Danish Ballet move together in such faultless accord? No, because they have been moving together since they were seven or eight years old. The same would be true of the Kirov or the Bolshoi or the Paris Opera Ballet and, to a degree, of Britain's Royal Ballet. A lifetime of dance can be passed within any one of these from seven to seventy areas of training and performing.

This does seem the ideal way but it does have one flaw. Although any such academy-theater encourages individuality and produces it, those who are somewhat less than a Bruhn or Kronstam, Fonteyn or Dowell, Plisetskaya or Vasiliev, Sizova or Soloviev, are not possessed of the imagination and drive to explore and experiment and dare. They need exposure to more dance ways than they learn at home.

In America, dancers "shop around." They go to a variety of schools and teachers, and often they find contrasting methods of instruction not only stimulating but enormously helpful. True, ballet technique is fairly standard the world around, but there are many methods of teaching it—a Bournonville method in Denmark, a Vaganova method in Leningrad, a Cecchetti method, and so on. This does not mean that steps are changed but simply that styles and routines of instruction may vary.

In the United States, there are a very few places where it is possible for the young student to receive both academic and dance instruction at the same school. New York City's High School of Performing Arts is unique. It is a public school—there is no tuition— and its students receive a high school education while majoring in dance, music or drama. The students are selected annually (they must be residents of New York) by audition. The applicants, who have completed elementary school or junior high elsewhere in the city, are initially screened by members of the HSPA faculty. In dance, once the hopelessly unsuited (usually for physical reasons) are weeded out, then members of the school's Advisory Commission (composed of dance critics, dance editors, senior dance teachers and choreographers, etc.) come in to pass judgment on the rest in a series of auditions which last two days.

At these auditions, the applicants are given exercises in ballet and in modern dance to do for the judges, and then each is permitted to do a dance of his own (or one that a private dance teacher has arranged for him). Senior dance students of the HSPA demonstrate the steps and movements called out by a faculty member. The applicants try to duplicate these actions as closely as possible. Some of the youngsters have had no previous dance training, some have had excellent training in private studios, others have received faulty instruction, some know only tap or, perhaps, Spanish dance and nothing of ballet or modern dance. All these factors are considered by the judges when rating each applicant.

Once accepted, the new student receives not only his academic training in courses required by the Board of Education but also full dance instruction under a faculty composed of professional dance people. The word "professional" is important, because dance courses in many colleges and universities are conducted by those who are products of educational dance training and who are, in turn, training others to be dance teachers in public school systems and colleges. Dance techniques employed may be similar or even identical, but the difference lies in "purpose."

The purpose of dance training at the High School of Performing Arts is to turn out performers, dancers who can earn a living in this vocation. And the record of success is remarkable, for more than ninety percent of the dance graduates go into paying dance jobs immediately upon, and sometimes prior to, graduation. There are jobs for them in ballet companies, in modern dance troupes, in musicals, in television, in summer theaters, in dance camps with summertime student productions, in nightclubs, in stage shows (such as at the Radio City Music Hall) and in any of a number of outlets.

To be ready for such job opportunities, the students at the High School of Performing Arts are given a dance program of three or four years duration (depending on their admittance time) which concentrates on ballet and modern dance. Pupils must take both techniques at the start, but in junior and senior years they may concentrate on the style of their choice. One may pick ballet; another, modern dance. But the point is that in the commercial world of dance they will never find themselves ignorant of any form.

Supplementary dance studies include ethnic dance techniques, such as Spanish or East Indian, plus tap or jazz or character dance. And character dance, which covers such historic and standard dances as the polka, the czardas, the mazurka and the like, is not to be taken lightly. Mary Skeaping, onetime ballet mistress of Britain's Royal Ballet and the Royal Swedish Ballet, loves to tell the tale of the time, right after World War II, when she was asked to produce the first classical ballet for British television. With the rehearsal time allotted to her, she concentrated on the pirouettes, the jetés, the lifts and other ballet virtuosities, and left a minimum of time for rehearsal of a waltz, only to discover that her dancers could pirouette with the best of them but did not know the rudiments of the waltz!

Now what, one may ask, is so important about a waltz or a czardas? Well, our graduate may get a job in a ballet company, but it is not at all certain that he or she will immediately be given elaborate classical enchaînement to accomplish. The great classics, such as *Swan Lake,* or *The Sleeping Beauty* or *Coppélia,* have their national dances, and the newcomer would do well to be prepared with anything from a schottische to a jota. Ted Shawn has found that his *Sixteen Dances in Sixteen Rhythms* is invaluable to the student dancer, preparing him to step out and count traditional dances which can turn up anywhere from ballet to TV.

At the High School of Performing Arts, these perennial character dances and national dances—some are regional and others, such as gypsy dances, are theatrical adaptations of rhythms rooted in a particular people—are taught because they are an essential to dance education.

But these character dances have their sources in Europe, in Western culture. What of the Orient? Our heritage now turns as easily and as logically to the East as to the West. So it is that at the High School of Performing Arts there are those students who are as interested in a Hindu sundari as they are in a heel-clicking czardas. What is their training in this area? One of their instructors has been Matteo, an American of Italian descent and a onetime pupil of La Meri, another American who has become one of the world's great authorities on the ethnic dance arts.

Matteo taught the interested HSPA students the dance forms of India, using his own teaching method which had earlier been approved by leading Indian dancers themselves. (In fact, an American method of teaching Indian dance, which is an art form thousands of years old, had been incorporated into the curriculum of one of India's most respected dance academies.) Matteo organized an Indo-American student group which absorbed not only technical aspects of Indian dance, Bharata Natyam, Kathakali, Kathak, Manipuri (the four major schools of Indian dance), but also the Sanskrit terminology and the profound philosophies which go with these ancient dances.

This extensive description of the High School of Performing Arts is given simply because it represents an ideal method of education for the youngster determined to become a professional dancer and because it is the closest thing the United States has to the national academies of Europe. There are, however, changes and developments in America's ballet training scene. In Washington, D.C., the Washington School of Ballet, headed by Mary Day, provides pupils with both academic and dance training, with the accent on ballet. The same is true of the National School of Ballet, in New York, headed by Thalia Mara. Others are slowly emerging.

There are, of course, ballet schools from coast to coast that serve related ballet companies. The School of American Ballet feeds newcomers into the New York City Ballet; the Ballet Theatre School for the American Ballet Theatre; the American Ballet Center for the City Center Joffrey Ballet; Harkness House for the Harkness Ballet, etc.

But in the main, the young American with a dance bent gets his formal schooling at one place and his ballet training at another.

How to decide what dance school to attend? Parents, who have not had a dance education themselves, are in no position to select, with infallibility, a good school and a good teacher. Few states require licensing, and those that do are more concerned with the physical facilities of the building itself—ventilation, toilets, fire escapes and the like—than with the caliber of a teacher. Indeed, who in a governmental licensing bureau would know a good ballet teacher from a bad one? Anyone can teach ballet as far as legality goes, although the teacher may never have had a lesson in his life. Suppose he or she teaches ballroom dancing and there is a sudden local interest in ballet; the ballroom teacher can buy a few books or, perhaps, even go to some sort of a big dance convention for a few days and institute ballet classes!

The ignorant parent, the unknowing student, are common prey to such charlatans.

So what to do? A rather hit-or-miss but workable procedure is for the parent and the prospective student to find out where ballet artists of national repute themselves study. They would not attend classes where instruction is bad. In New York or in other big cities, this is easy to do. But what about a smaller community? Professional ballet companies tour, and when they stop off for a performance in a community, many of the dancers visit local schools "to take class." They have learned from dancers who toured before them just where the best place is to go.

The emergence of regional ballet companies, semiprofessional but usually groups with good technical and esthetic standards, has helped raise the level of ballet instruction across the United States. These community ballets, each the product of a local dance school, join regional ballet associations and apply to take part in the annual regional ballet festivals which may be held in the Southeast (the oldest such group), the Pacific Northwest (one of the newest) or elsewhere. All such groups have agreed to have outside professionals (with no local commitments) serve as adjudicators, and these highly experienced critics and teachers visit all of the member schools in a given region, see all the ballets submitted for the annual regional ballet festival, select out of many the best companies and the best productions to assure a stirring, provocative festival.

A by-product, and an important one it is, of such festivals is that local teachers, local choreographers and local students come together and find out what the others are doing. They see where they are weak and where they are strong, they are exposed (even briefly) to different training methods, and they return home, both teachers and pupils, with greater ballet knowledge and greater determination than they had before. This side of the regional ballet movement has to do with education, and it is of vast importance to the potential dancers of tomorrow.

Membership in regional ballet enterprises does not automatically mean a high level of ballet instruction. Almost any school company can pay membership dues and join a regional ballet association, granted certain essentials. But membership does not promise selection for festival events. When the adjudicators arrive, the inferior units in the membership are going to be eliminated from the festivals. Parents and their dance-minded children can find plenty of valuable clues right here to areas of first-rate ballet instruction.

But, and it is a large one, some ballet teachers are not interested in ballet companies, in forming one or running one. They are interested only in teaching. In the quiet of the classroom they excel. So one must look closely to find the dedicated, knowledgeable instructor in any community, large or small. It is not always easy. The local studio with the largest enrollment and the biggest advertising may be the worst place to study ballet. Ironically, it may be the best. Visit the schools, look at the classes, find out who goes there, what graduates went on to fame and fortune? Observe.

If you don't know what to look for, how can you observe? Well, let's take one item in the field of ballet, dancing on pointe. What does the local teacher do about it and, more important, *when?*

It is not possible to set an exact age when the child can go on toe, but it is possible to state the approximate age, and that would be nine years old. For a few, eight might be safe; for others, eleven. The development of the child has much to do with it. If the growing bones are still soft, the pointe must be postponed until greater maturity is reached. But the most important consideration is the period of ballet training provided before the student uses toe shoes.

Just as ballet existed for hundreds of years before dancing on pointe was introduced, so today's pupil must mirror in her own training the same metamorphosis. Two years of *daily* instruction in basic ballet technique should precede the introduction of pointe work. Some schools permit the use of pointe after one year of daily lessons, but then only if the child is old enough and strong enough for this new challenge.

The majority of today's ballerinas suggest two to two and one-half years of intensive ballet training before using pointe. Do these essential rules prevail at the studio your child is attending? If not, watch out for inferior dance instruction at all levels.

Very often, the teacher is not wholly to blame for putting a little girl into toe shoes too soon. Mothers are the worst offenders, for in their ignorance they think that ballet is "toe" and that if little Susie is not doing toe dancing, she isn't dancing. There are many knowledgeable teachers who put little girls into toe shoes too quickly because of competition: "I know it's wrong," they'll say, "but if I don't do it, the mothers will take their children around the corner to a teacher who will put them on pointe. I not only lose a customer but am also guilty of turning over a child to an instructor who knows far less about ballet than I. Toe shoes at a tender age are wrong, but maybe, because I know the body, I can minimize the dangers."

And are there dangers? Of course there are. The very least one could expect from dancing on pointe too soon is ugly legs. Mother, of course, has decided that dancing will make her little one graceful—and properly taught, it would do just that—but she doesn't realize that improper pointe training will lead to knotty calves, unlovely and uncomfortable bunions and related deformities. At the worst, toe dancing at an immature period can cause jointal injuries, such as water on the knee, and injuries to ankles, toes and even hips. Does the teacher in your community recognize these dangers?

But this has to do with toe dancing. What about the age to start non-pointe dance instruction? That can begin at almost any age. Children are born to dance, they are born to move, and they almost always respond to music with waves of the arms, crawls and investigative steps. Martha Graham believes that they should have no formal dance instruction when they are little. "Just turn on the phonograph, let them dress up in whatever their imagination tells them to, and leave them alone. They'll dance."

Isadora Duncan, when she was barely a toddler herself, organized dance classes for babies too young to walk. They simply waved their arms in rhythm and loved it.

Today, the little ones can play dance games, imitate animals in movement, step to rounds (such as "Three Blind Mice") and have fun while they are learning simple disciplines. Modern dance is probably the best technique to promote easy and early disciplines. But ballet, *without* toe shoes, can begin safely at seven or eight.

Why modern dance (or games or folk dances) and not ballet for babies? Modern dance stems from the natural movements of the human body; ballet's premise is unnatural, it is contrived in order to achieve a very special style of movement. Perhaps the best way to put it is that one can begin to dance in modern dance technique at the very start of training. With ballet, one has to master a foreign language.

It is not simply that the technical terminology of ballet is in French. It is that in modern dance, a skip, hop, run, walk, jump, fall and the like are the ingredients of dance action. In ballet, there must be the turnout of the limbs, the mastery of the five positions of the feet, the command of port de bras, the special placement of the body *before* you can translate a walk, run, leap, jump, turn into dancing. Your muscles must learn a foreign movement tongue in order to speak in dance.

So ballet training may begin at seven or eight—the age

used by most of the royal and state ballet schools of Europe —but the teacher not only does not use pointe work at such a time but avoids pressing young bodies into extreme turn-outs of the limbs. That can come gradually.

In European ballet schools and in certain ones in America, boys and girls are separated for their classes. Although the fundamental dance technique remains the same, the difference between the male and female physiques governs differences in movement. Even when separate classes are not held, at the closing period of a given class the teacher usually divides the class by sexes and gives the girls pointe exercises and the boys essays in leaps, jumps and air turns. However, the desirable way is to have separate classes so that even in strictly stylized port de bras, the delicacy of the female is not allowed to influence the stronger arm movements of the men. In an American ballet class, the closing ten or fifteen minutes of a one-and-one-half-hour class are given over to this separation. Otherwise, the girls would have an hour class of pointe work and the boys their own special class. The two sexes, of course, must work together in adagio classes, in the art of partnering.

If dancing is to be merely avocational, two lessons a week will suffice to sustain interest and to initiate some progress. One lesson per week is useless except as an introduction to appreciation for an art form. One lesson a week for the child-beginner is all right, but if a career is planned and dancing as a vocation is selected, then daily study must be pursued. And it never, never stops.

The professional ballet dancer, even the prima ballerina and the premier danseur, never omits daily classes, except briefly during a very short annual vacation or when sick or injured. The standard practice, when a ballet season is on or the company on tour, is for the dancer to take a morning class at a studio of his own selection and then, about an hour or two before curtain-time at the theater, take a company class or warm-up. It is not necessary before a performance for the dancer to take a complete class—the stretches at the ballet barre, the adagios in center, the elaborate turns and leaps in various combinations. The barre is usually enough. Although if the ballerina is going to have to do an extended series of turns, such as the thirty-two fouettés, she will probably practice them. She and her partner will also rehearse at

Ballet Barre

the last minute tricky lifts or other supports involving exact timings.

As the dancer grows older, the daily lessons seem harder. And they are. For the body, physically, begins to deteriorate in its twenties! The dancer fights the inroads of time and retains the accomplishments made by a young body long after the average person could retain similar physical prowess in other areas.

But even if it becomes more difficult each day to raise the leg to the same height it was raised yesterday or last year, and even if the average dancer finds an ache somewhere in the body at every waking and sleeping moment, body tone and the figure as well as muscular accomplishment are retained way past middle age. It is a hard life and a disciplined life which the dancer leads, but if longevity is one of the goals, most dancers achieve it.

The daily routine is the same, although the specific ingredients and accents and stresses may vary from day to day, from teacher to teacher. For a lifetime, the professional ballet artist may go into a classroom in New York, Cedar Rapids, Dallas, Copenhagen, Moscow, Tokyo and be quite at home as the teacher calls out instructions in French, as the class goes from the kneebends (in the five positions), the rond-de-jambes (on the ground and in the air), the battements (small and large), the developés, the relevés, the balances, all of the stretches and controls, at barre to the first center work, which repeats or at least echoes the barre work but without the support of the barre, and then moves in to traveling exercises, to combinations and enchaînements which pull together the plot, plan, sequence and development of the entire class. Variety, of course, is possible within this pattern. One day, the teacher may use as a classroom leit motif turns of all sorts; another time, balances; again, adagio type movements, slow and sustained; again, all manner of batterie, of leg-beats.

The star dancer, no matter how famous, when attending class obeys the teacher. Certainly, the teacher is not going to correct a great ballerina in a loud voice; it will be done quietly and unobtrusively, but the correction, the suggestion will be made. At the close of a class, even the world's most illustrious stars will turn to the instructor, bow, and if she is a female teacher, say, "Thank you, Madame." Ballet was born in a world of etiquette in the royal courts of centuries ago, and it has not forgotten polite behavior.

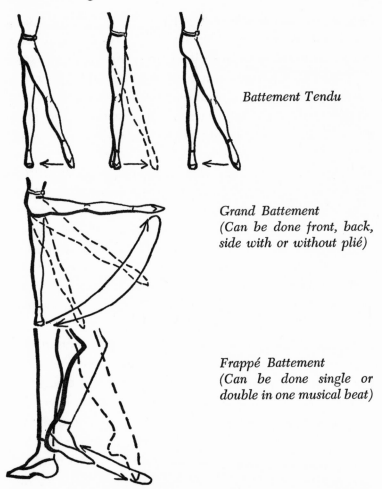

Battement Tendu

Grand Battement
*(Can be done front, back,
side with or without plié)*

Frappé Battement
*(Can be done single or
double in one musical beat)*

When a ballerina or a danseur feels that extra coaching is needed, he or she will go for private lessons with a teacher skilled in whatever styles or special disciplines are desired. It is possible for a veteran dancer to find that turns are somehow going awry, and if the dancer cannot correct it himself or in his regular class, he will go for a special coaching lesson.

Coaching is even more common with respect to roles. A ballerina may have won acclaim in a contemporary repertory and then find herself with an opportunity to perform in *Giselle* or *The Sleeping Beauty*. She may go to an old-time teacher or to a retired ballerina of the classical school in order to be instructed in every step, arm movement, phrasing, gesture of a role. Maybe the ballerina knows one version of, say, *The Nutcracker*, and then is invited as guest artist to appear with a company which has a somewhat different version of the old classic; then, she may go to a coach who knows the version in question or ask the director or régisseur of the troupe to outline her role in the version with which she is not yet familiar.

The danseur or the ballerina, despite star status, every now and again takes a beginners' ballet class. This is in order to go back to fundamentals (which occur in classes of all levels) but taken very slowly and with patience and extra analysis.

Although the old ballet masterpieces may be constant in the world's ballet repertories, popular preferences change and influence even the old classics. Perhaps dancers have more bravura in one decade than in another or are more realistic or more lyrical. The steps don't change, as a rule, but attitudes and attacks do. Sometimes, old-fashioned mime sequences are dropped for years at a time, and suddenly they seem charming as well as quaint and there is a move to restore them. Good examples are the mimed episodes in *Giselle* and *Swan Lake*.

Britain's Royal Ballet restored (and other companies have followed suit), the fairly elaborate mime scene in Act II of

Swan Lake in which Odette explains through traditional gesture that she is in the toils of an evil magician, that the lake the Prince sees was made from her mother's flowing tears and that she, Odette, shall never be freed until one man comes along and promises, forsaking all others, to wed her and be eternally true to her. It is old-fashioned but it is lovely.

In *Giselle* in Act I, the Mother does not warn Giselle against dancing because of her delicacy, but in the restored mime scene she tells her daughter of evil forces at work, of ghost maidens who dance in cemeteries at night, of the implacable Queen of the Wilis. In order to bring back these almost forgotten scenes, artists of an earlier era were invited to coach the artists of today in the execution of such scenes. For the Royal Ballet, it was the great Tamara Karsavina, whose memory went back to the Russian Imperial Ballet.

If the dancer needs to be coached in the ways of the past, he also needs training in new ways of movement. In the strict ballet classroom, he will get neither modern dance nor jazz. Yet new ballets draw from such sources. Even a ballerina, if she wishes to extend her repertory, will relish the challenge of, say, a ballet with jazz flavors, and to prepare herself for the assignment, she will attend jazz classes.

Study of old styles, study of new ways, study and restudy of the body, constitute a way of life for the dancer. For the female dancer, a baby can interrupt this course of study, but it is not permitted to interfere.

A ballerina usually performs through the early months of her pregnancy, unless, of course, her doctor finds reasons for her to refrain from any action whatsoever. And after she leaves the stage—because of her appearance and not because of health—she will continue to take daily class almost to the day of the birth. Toward the close of such a period, she will forego pointe work, eliminate jumps and drop other extreme exercises, but she will do a modest barre.

After the baby is born, the ballerina-mother begins almost immediately to restore muscle tone and strength to her body. Melissa Hayden, for example, lies in her hospital bed right after the birth and starts to raise and lower her legs to regain instant control over the once distended, and now flattened, abdomen. In a matter of hours, she is standing by the bed and doing a few barre exercises. This is not as wild as it sounds; in many primitive societies there are prenatal dances for pregnant women in order to assure easy delivery. Deep kneebends serve both ballet and motherhood.

This ballet life, predicated upon continuing dedication, what is it like? Well, we have seen that it is a lifelong assignment involving daily dance duties. If it doesn't follow this pattern, it fails. But can it be normal? Yes. Most dancers are married, and they learn how to make a home life fit in with a studio and stage life. If both husband and wife are dancers, which they often are, the daily schedule doesn't seem strange to either. Grandma, a baby-sitter or a friend can watch the littlest one while the parents are practicing, rehearsing, performing. And at tour time, the baby usually goes on the road too. He doesn't mind. He naps in the prompter's box or the wings, he looks at the gorgeous lights, and his parents are close. As the little one gets older, he or she becomes something of a critic. The daughter of Mia Slavenska, the Yugoslav-born ballerina, once remarked to her mother as the star left the stage, "Not bad, but your fouettés were a little off." And Yuriko, a principal with Martha Graham, heard her daughter say, "You dance very nice, Mommy, but Miss Graham is better."

Dancers will dance anywhere there is what Miss Graham would call a "Dancing-Ground." It may be grubby, dirty, hot, cold, ancient, uncomfortable, but it is where dancing lives. Stages vary around the world, and the artists of the ballet must adapt themselves to stages which are narrow or deep or raked or uneven, slick or rough, splintered or pitted.

Studios are no different. Dancers are used to going to drab old buildings where dust flies up when they land from a jump or where the ceilings are so low that, in a lift, they could crack their heads on a cross-beam. They take such hazards with equanimity. But there are also good studios— airy, desirable flooring, spacious, even luxurious.

There are, for example, beautiful classrooms for ballet in the New York State Theater at Lincoln Center or in the headquarters of the Washington School of Ballet. These compare quite favorably with facilities available at the Royal Theater in Copenhagen and in other nationally sponsored ballet centers. Topping even such government-sponsored institutions is the Harkness House for Ballet Arts in New York City. Here, a great city mansion has been made over into a school where the necessities of the ideal classroom for dance are combined with luxurious appointments which attract the eye and feed esthetic needs.

The student or the star, then, can go to a dingy room where there are dirty windows and a tinny, cigarette-scarred piano and a teacher, and he will polish his art there. Or, perhaps, he will go to Harkness House, or its nearest equivalent, and find pleasant surroundings and additional stimuli. At Harkness House, for example, he will have classes in many aspects of ballet, courses in modern dance, in ethnic forms, in music for the dance, in design. There will be a dance library of books and of musical recordings at his disposal. There will be workshops and art exhibits featuring great paintings and sculptures inspired by dance.

But wherever the ballet student goes—a gloomy walkup to a trashy studio or an elevator to a gorgeously appointed studio—he will get to work. One is far better than the other, *but* the future, *his* future, is contained in his own body.

Chapter 7

Interpretation and Individuality

If the ballet steps and gestures mastered in the classroom are going to have any meaning on stage, they must be treated rather like "movement words." If they are to evoke any response from an audience, they must have something to say. Color, stress, accent, timing, sharpness, softness, slowness, speed and placements of the head and limbs are among the numberless factors which give eloquence to otherwise meaningless steps.

An English-speaking actress, for example, uses the English tongue to interpet the roles in which she appears. The words are pretty much the same for each role, although the order is, of course, different. The playwright, naturally, selects English words suitable, say, for the character of Lady Bracknell in *The Importance of Being Earnest,* and the same playwright (Oscar Wilde) also uses English, but in a different selection, for the innocent heroine of the same play. The actress takes it from there.

In *Romeo and Juliet,* the actor knows that playing Mercutio is quite different from playing Romeo or Tybalt, for although the words are in English, it is the way they are sung, whispered, shouted, spat out, insinuated, declaimed, projected, which have a great deal to do with the defining of a specific character.

The same is true in ballet.

Princess Aurora in *The Sleeping Beauty* and Odette in *Swan Lake* do arabesques, pirouettes, bourrées, jetés and most of the standard steps, but the secret is that they do not permit them to be standard. Aurora's arabesque is that of a happy sixteen-year-old poised on the threshold of life; Odette's arabesque is that of an enchanted birdlike creature floating in space. In frozen silhouette they might look almost identical, but seen in movement—that is, the preparation for the arabesque, the going into it, the way of holding it, the manner of resolving it—they are as different as the two characters themselves.

Within *Swan Lake* itself there are passages which are almost identical for Odette and Odile. Indeed, they were so designed that the Prince might be misled into believing that the villainous Odile was actually Odette. But the public must not be confused for one second. The audience must be able to see a harshness of attack in the way Odile moves, and when she is literally imitating the swanlike arms of Odette, we must see the predatory cast to the tilt of her head, the duplicity in her very stance. Great ballerinas achieve this.

But great ballerinas go further; they are not only different as Odette and as Odile, but they are different from each other. If they were not, the balletomane would not go back to see again and again the most popular of all ballets, *Swan Lake*. As a dance critic for more than a quarter of a century,

I have seen more *Swan Lakes* than I can count, either the four-act staging or the ever-popular one-acter (Act II). Frequently, I am called upon to see a good many of them during a given ballet season, even as many as five four-acters in a row (Friday night and Saturday afternoon and night and Sunday afternoon and night). That, I might point out, is an awful lot of Tchaikovsky and feathers (about sixteen hours) to take in such a short span of time. I must do it because of major cast changes, such as five sets of Odettes-Odiles and Siegfrieds. And what makes it bearable, and very often exciting, is that no two ballerinas are the same. The steps are the same but the ways in which they do them are totally different.

Odette is a girl, a princess and an enchanted swan. All of these characteristics must be present in the interpretation of the role. But shifts in accent are possible and desirable. One ballerina may center her interpretation upon the girl-woman, upon the feminine aspects of the part; another stresses the regality of a handsome queen; still another will find the flutterings of a bird the key to the ballet. All are valid.

But what of Odile? Well, she can do the thirty-two fouettés in the coda of the third-act pas de deux simply as a tour de force, just as a coloratura soprano can do a cadenza and a trill as a vocal gymnastic or as a bird or a bell. She can also do the thirty-two fouettés as a mesmeric dazzle to capture and conquer the attention of the Prince. She can dance the role of Odile, the Black Swan, as if she were malevolent herself and relished her magical powers, or she can dance it as if she were merely an instrument of evil, subject to the commands of Von Rothbart, her magician-father who is responsible for Odette's transformation.

The possibilities in characterization, even through age-old ballet steps and gestures, are endless.

How could anyone presume that Odette would move as Odile? Or Princess Aurora like the peasant Swanilda? Or the fragile Giselle like the blazing Kitri in *Don Quixote*. But look, and you will see that many of the steps are the same. When grandma says, "I love you," to her tousled-headed grandchild, she means it; when Romeo says it to Juliet, he means it; when couples say, "I love you," on their wedding night and on their fiftieth wedding anniversary, they mean it. But is the inflection the same? The words are, but is not one excited and anticipatory and another mellow and fond? One expectant and another grateful? The same is true of movements in dance.

If there is incredible variety possible for interpretations within classical ballet itself, just think of the scope offered by ballets incorporating modern or ethnic flavors. There are lovely turns in "attitude" in *Giselle*, turns which suggest the buoyancy of an exuberant lass. In *Pillar of Fire*, the ballerina does arabesque turns—different from attitudes only in that the knee is not bent—but here she does the movement as if it were a desperate method of escape from all the sordid, lonely, tragic feelings that well up within her.

Lizzie Borden does turns in arabesque in *Fall River Legend* just before she takes up an ax to kill her parents. You will find arabesque turns in ballets which are gay, sad or without plot at all. Obviously, this ancient step must be done differently for each occasion.

In addition to the demands of character—Odette, Odile, Lizzie Borden, Swanilda, the female insect in *The Cage,* Columbine, Giselle, the tormented bride in *Lilac Garden*—the ballerina must think of style. You just don't dance *La Sylphide* of the 1830's as you dance *The Sleeping Beauty* of the 1890's or *Agon* of the 1960's. You just don't. Yet the basic steps are the same.

A role makes its special demands; so does an age. The Romantic Age of ballet asks a softness, a gentleness, of the female which is not to be found in the more bravura roles of a century later. The danseur is a prince, a cavalier in one age, an importunate male in another, a hood in still another. The gentle Albrecht in *Giselle* does pirouettes. The violent Stanley in *A Streetcar Named Desire* also does pirouettes. Are they alike? Just about as alike as a "Yes" and a "Yeah."

Let us take a look at *La Sylphide* and Balanchine's *Agon* or *Episodes*. What are the differences? The five positions of the feet are present in both. Port de bras is there. The art of ballet is equally apparent in both. But the art of song is equally apparent in Joan Sutherland singing an aria from *Lucia di Lamermoor* and Ethel Merman belting out "You Cain't Get a Man with a Gun." Notes, pitch, rhythm are the ingredients of both. Ballet has its equivalent diversities.

La Sylphide, which the Royal Danish Ballet has preserved for more than a century, is a perfect example of romantic style. There is a softness to a leap not found in ballets of other periods, the arms have a softness also, and the use of the head suggests an ever-so-delicate archness. Looking at *La Sylphide* today, you can't help seeing images of old lithographs depicting Taglioni in her greatest role, and perhaps you wonder if today's ballet masters or régisseurs try to have their dancers copy the quaint old lithographs. Anton Dolin, in his lovely *Pas de Quatre*, actually incorporated poses from such lithographs into his choreography, but remember that no matter how fanciful the artists of that romantic day may have been, they were also reporting, and their paintings and lithographs thus recorded a style of dance for a special period in ballet history.

If the manner, steps and forms of the Romantic Age of ballet were recorded only by the written word, the sweet lithograph and memories passed along from one generation to another, today's ballet age has better methods of recording the movements of dance.

Dance notation, or dance script, is not new. Indeed, it goes back to the very beginnings of ballet. But as ballet grew, dance scripts could not keep up with all the innovations in step, movement, gesture. Terminology—arabesque, pas de chat, sauté—would define a step, but it could not state where it was done with respect to other dancers, or in what direction, or whether the movement was big or small, sharp or delicate.

Dance scripts, therefore, were essential to extend a record of a ballet further than terminology could do, and, in modern times, to extend that record beyond ballet itself. Notation systems have included methods involving stick figures on a floor plan of action, stick figures on a music staff (placed along with appropriate musical notes), spiral designs recording successive dance actions, and innumerable other approaches.

Today, Labanotation is the preferred method in America and in many parts of the world. Originated by the great German modern dance pioneer, Rudolf von Laban, and refined, renewed and constantly up-dated by the American dance notation expert, Ann Hutchinson, and her colleagues both in America and in Europe, Labanotation can record with accuracy any movement in any style, including the nine movements of the eyeball in Hindu dance. Labanotation, then, records, literally, the flutter of an eyelid. Great Britain's Royal Ballet prefers the less complex Benesh system, an excellent shorthand for recording choreography, but one which presupposes knowledge of ballet as a guideline for translating a Benesh score into action.

Movies, of course, are another sure way of recording a work of choreography for posterity. Films also make a record of performing attributes as well as of choreographic pattern and, in reviving an old work, the personal styles of given performers might be intrusive. Hence, a combination of the cold, exact script provided by Labanotation, and the film record is ideal for dance reconstructions. We can only guess at the exact steps and patterns of ballet used during the Romantic Age; tomorrow's reconstructors need have no qualms about how we choreographed and danced in the mid 1900's— it is there on film and in Labanotation.

But speaking of the Romantic Age of ballet, how should *Giselle* be played? Obviously, it must be in the romantic cast, that is, gentle rather than strident, poetic rather than dramatic. Now that may seem to be an odd thing to say, for does not *Giselle* culminate its first act in a Mad Scene which requires the ballerina to communicate her moods through acting as well as in dance?

Nora Kaye, who had criticized herself for being "too clinical," added that she could not conceive of the role of the peasant maid Giselle as a vehicle for "a ballerina slumming."

What she was referring to was the tendency of most ballerinas to perform the part of Giselle with an elegance rooted in the foundations of ballet itself, the royal court. Miss Kaye was correct on both counts, but not entirely, for *Giselle* was created in a period when the ballerina was called "the queen of the dance" and when drama was an essential ingredient of any ballet. How to reconcile the regal ballerina with a simple peasant girl? Today's great ballerinas do not conceal their ballerina-hood with respect to the execution of classical steps, but in their acting, they endeavor to make the onlooker believe in the simple girl who places her trust in a handsome youth, who is deceived by him, who goes mad from shock, who dies.

Miss Kaye, in the ballet which made her a sensational star overnight, *Pillar of Fire*, prepared for the role for two years. She knew more about the character of Hagar than anyone ever saw, literally, on stage, but what she knew about the unseen woman made the stage figure a heroine of blazing force.

Take the walk of the male dancer. As the Prince in *Swan Lake*, he walks (in Act I) among his guests with grace, ease and what might be described as "royal condescension." As the slave in *Scheherazade*, he slinks; as a Tartar in *Prince Igor*, he stalks; as Harlequin, he always prances; as Stanley in *Streetcar*, he swaggers; as the old king in *Bluebeard*, he totters; as one of the lads in *Interplay*, he can saunter with loose hips; as the returning, penitent Prodigal in *Prodigal Son*, he walks humbly on his knees to his father.

The walk is just one example of the need for a vast array of accents in a vast array of roles. The arms, the head, the neck, the torso will all be used differently from style to style, from ballet to ballet, from role to role, from scene to scene, from measure to measure, from step to step.

The ballerina and the danseur each not only need to invest his own separate movements with style and meaning but must also establish an interlocking relationship with respect to movement. In many passages within a ballet, they must move together in perfect physical accord. But this is just the start, for they must establish a rapport, going beyond mere motor timing, with respect to style (both period and per-

Supported Adage

sonal), dynamic accent and the degree of dramatics involved.

The art of partnering, on the purely physical basis, requires sensitivity, sometimes almost to the point of ESP, on the part of both artists. Suppose the ballerina is standing on one pointe, perhaps in arabesque or attitude or even in the simplest position of all with one leg drawn up slightly to touch the foot of the lifted leg to the ankle of the standing leg. The male dancer does not attempt to place the female dancer on balance—only she knows the exactitude of the plumb line through her body which will keep her poised—but he does provide her with a strong arm and a steady hand, and it is *she* who finds her own balance with this support so that when she lets go (and it is *she* who withdraws her hand at the right moment), she can maintain her balance, alone, for the maximum length of time.

A supported pirouette is somewhat different. Usually, the ballerina generates her own momentum and spins within the encircling (around the waist) hands of her partner until his hands, at the right instant, press in and stop her. Is there anything else that the man can do? Yes, he must know exactly when to stop her, and I don't mean simply when she is full-face to the audience (or, if the choreography requires it, with back to the audience ready for a sudden back bend as in the Adagio of Act II of *Swan Lake*). He must sense, through tactile responses and through a judging of her speed and through the degree of retention of her verticality, just how long she can turn. The number of turns will vary, not only from day to day, but from sequence to sequence. The danseur must feel this and bring the pirouettes to a conclusion at the perfect second.

If the ballerina strays a bit from verticality while doing a supported turn, the cavalier can ease her back to uprightness, imperceptibly if he is an experienced partner. Some female dancers like assistance with controlling their momentum in a supported turn, and for those who require this extra aid, the male dancer, placing his hands slightly below her waist and on the hips, will give her a sendoff, rather as if he were pulling the string on a top. Perhaps she needs this outside force more at the close of the turn than at its beginning to fill out a musical phrase. But most ballerinas dispense with this aspect of partnering.

When it comes to lifts—that is, the elevating of the female dancer by the male above his head or to one side or in holds close to the floor or in catches—the male does most of the work, muscularly speaking. But the female can help. Her timing must coincide with his, and in upward lifts, she can help by giving a subtly concealed pushoff from the floor and by breathing properly (just an intake of breath lifts the body). And if she is to run across the stage and, in horizontal flight, hurtle into her partner's waiting arms (a dazzling trick beloved by the dancers of the Bolshoi Ballet), her timing had better be good—or else!

Perfect timing and perfect placement are not achieved by instinct alone. Practice and testing are essential. Since no two dancers are exactly alike in size, in technique, in style and in motor response, adjustments must be made every time there is an exchange of partners. Basically, it is the man who adjusts to the woman, for he provides his strength and his presence where and when she needs it. Details of such adjustments may seem small but they are important, for they make for security. In a lift, for example, the ballerina may ask the danseur to hold her a fraction lower down on the hip than his preceding ballerina wanted. Or, perhaps, in a support involving only the hands, she may wish him to hold her by the wrist or even by the lower arm. The length of the arm, the height of the performers, the resolution of the step itself (it might go from a balance into a quick pirouette) affect the necessary physical-muscular relationship between two performers.

Backstage, just before the house lights dim, the last bit of practice you are likely to see on stage, before the artists take their places, will involve a boy and a girl giving a final test to *that* difficult lift, *that* tricky supported pirouette, *that* unusual balance.

But there is far more to the art of partnering than physical prowess and sensitiveness. There must be rapport with respect to dramatic projection (if it is a narrative ballet to be danced) and style. Again, it is the danseur who adjusts to the ballerina, although the ballerina may well be inspired by the special artistry of her cavalier and color her own interpretation accordingly.

Let us take an example of esthetic adjustments in partnering. The recently retired Alexandra Danilova and Alicia Markova could and occasionally did share the same danseur for certain roles, but did he partner them alike? How could he! Danilova, the exuberant, tempestuous, often humorous, regal, intensely feminine artist; Markova, tiny, wistful, ethereal, remote, seemingly as fragile as thistledown. With Markova, the danseur would tone down his dramatics, make gentle his displays of ardor, touch her and glance at her as if she were almost a vision. With Danilova, the thrust of drama would be greater, the ardor more fiery, and he would feast on her with his eyes. Both of these great ladies of the dance were incomparable artists and yet totally different from each other. A partner had to recognize this and perform accordingly.

England's Fonteyn, with her innocent radiance, and Russia's Plisetskaya, with her blazing presence, invite different support from the partner.

Even if the ballerina is usually the key to the tone and timbre of a special partnership, the male dancer also exerts his own influences. Fonteyn, when she first became associated with Rudolf Nureyev, took on a greater dynamic inten-

sity than she ever had before. There was more of the woman
and less of the innocent girl about her. The Russian escapee's
animal-like grace, his bravura stance, his moodiness and his
mystery affect all who surround him on stage. Silently, he
commands it, although he always heeds the special qualities
established by Fonteyn herself.

Erik Bruhn, the greatest premier danseur noble of the
mid-twentieth century, creates his own air of princeliness in
classical ballets, and junior ballerinas who dance with him
instinctively add a cloak of elegance to their own dramatic
dress. Yet, Bruhn, in such sensual ballets as *Carmen,* elicits
passionate responses from the ballerina who is assigned the
title role.

The men in classical ballet (if not in modern works) may
influence the performing of the females, but the pattern is
usually that of the behavior of a prince consort, for the ballerina is the reigning queen.

Partnerships may also involve something more than being
physically adept in moving together through the measures
of dance or even something more than an esthetic rapport.
A partnership which is more than a working one may evolve
into something known in show business as "a team." And a
team which sends forth sparks invariably captures the public's fancy and becomes, very often, a greater draw at the
box office than a single luminary.

The sense of "team" does not cheapen the partnership one
whit, for although it was long common in vaudeville, it
spilled over into all kinds of theatrical partnerships: Sothern
and Marlowe; Lunt and Fontanne; the movies' Fred Astaire
and Ginger Rogers or Jeanette MacDonald and Nelson Eddy;

Vernon and Irene Castle, who made ballroom dance history, and many more.

More than two hundred years ago, Marie Sallé found her brother to be her ideal partner until his untimely death; a century later, the vivacious Fanny Cerrito was half of a dazzling team with her husband (the marriage finally broke up), Arthur Saint-Léon.

In this century, ballet teams of the highest artistic standards have brought pleasure to the public. Karsavina and Nijinsky were not actually a team (in the sense that Fonteyn and Nureyev were to become decades later), but they danced frequently together and made performing history in ballets which themselves made history.

Later, in the 1930's and especially in the 1940's, came the electrifying team of Alexandra Danilova and Frederic Franklin. Both were ebullient by nature, both had a feel for the bravura and both projected, when suitable, bubbling humor. They danced classical ballets together and character works, having their greatest popular successes in the latter category which included *Coppélia, Le Beau Danube, Gaité Parisienne* at the top of the list. After years with the Ballet Russe de Monte Carlo as its foremost stars, this team continued to appear together as guest artists in companies, ensembles and simply duo events all over the world right up to Danilova's retirement from the stage.

Contemporary with Danilova and Franklin were Alicia Markova and Anton Dolin. Although the versatile Dolin would let his Irish ebullience (he was born Patrick Healey-Kay) burst forth in any number of roles, when dancing with the gentle Markova he was always the impeccable premier danseur, the solicitous cavalier, the tender gallant. Their *Giselle* (in Dolin's superb staging) was the finest in their era. Indeed, it was the definitive *Giselle* of the 1940's, and those who remember it well are certain that it will never be equaled by any other team. Markova and Dolin, of course, appeared in other classics during their years with the American Ballet Theatre and as directors of their own company (they had two periods with a Markova-Dolin ballet); and as ballet's most popular team (they even appeared in a Broadway show, such was their popular appeal), they traveled the world. Their careers followed divergent paths from time to time, but from the 1920's into the 1950's, the combination, Markova-Dolin, was magic.

For many years, in Britain's Royal Ballet (formerly the Sadler's Wells Ballet), Fonteyn's most constant partner was the handsome Michael Somes. It was an admirable duo but it was not quite a "team," for as much as Somes was admired, it was Fonteyn who was the undisputed star. Then, as Fonteyn entered her forties (and she had hinted at retirement), along came Nureyev, whose dancing with the Kirov Ballet in western Europe and whose dramatic escape into the arms of the French police hit the front pages of the newspapers. Fonteyn invited Nureyev to appear at a ballet gala with her. The rest is history. In his mid-twenties, Nureyev, with the unruly hair, the sullen expression (which could shift instantly into a radiant, boyish smile), the perfect body, the remarkable technique, became the partner of a woman old enough to be his mother, but a woman with the dewiness of youth about her and with a technique which, at forty, was better than it had ever been before.

Fonteyn-Nureyev, another historic ballet "team." At the

Royal Opera House, Covent Garden, London; at New York's Metropolitan Opera House, and in cities and towns around the world, "the hottest little team in show biz," which is how I described them irreverently in the New York *Herald Tribune* (and was picked up as a lead in *Life* magazine), held audiences enthralled.

Their joint artistry in *Swan Lake, Giselle,* Kenneth Mac-Millan's *Romeo and Juliet,* in Sir Frederick Ashton's *Marguerite and Armand* (created from the Camille story especially for them) or in such tours de force as the *Corsair* Pas de Deux was of such stature that critics as well as the public were left spellbound.

The Fonteyn-Nureyev team exerted its appeal beyond the actual dancing itself. In their lovely and skillfully calculated curtain calls, Dame Margot would curtsy to Nureyev, kiss a rose from her bouquet and hand it shyly to him. He, then, would lift her to her feet, kiss her hand rapturously and press the rose to his heart. This was pretty much the standard procedure at all performances, but audiences sighed and perhaps wondered if the romance they had seen danced in the ballet had not lingered after the performance. At that instant of romantic pleasure, they did not care that Dame Margot was happily married to another and was a devoted wife (on American tours, she often flew back to England during a break in her performing schedule just to be with her husband). Nor, at the moment of the tenderness displayed at the curtain calls, could the public think that their "Rudi" was footloose and fancy free.

American ballet, of course, has had its ballet teams. The American Ballet Theatre, in addition to Markova and Dolin, came up with a heady combination in the fiery Alicia Alonso and that dapper premier danseur of Russian heritage, Igor Youskevitch. They too had their triumphs in *Giselle*, and for a time, New York balletomanes formed separate camps (as did the highly partisan followers of Taglioni and Elssler), one hailing the younger team of Alonso-Yousekevitch, and the other singing the praises of their incomparable Markova-Dolin.

Maria Tallchief and the Danish-born Erik Bruhn became, for a brief period, enormously popular as a duo not only in ballet companies but as guest artists and as dance stars for television. Another Tallchief, sister Marjorie, and her husband, George Skibine, danced together in Europe for nearly twenty years (mainly at the Paris Opéra), until Skibine's retirement as a dancer.

Other great partnerships have contributed richly not only to the art of ballet itself but to that aura of romance which surrounds, or should, one of the most unashamedly romantic of all of the performing arts.

Not all of the glamorous, glittering and seemingly romantic partnerships were characterized by smooth sailing offstage as well as on. And sometimes, the sailing wasn't always smooth even on stage, for slips, near-misses and actual misses are inescapable in a performing art which requires the utmost in strength, dexterity, precision and timing. But slips and slides don't belong here—more of them in the next chapter.

Chapter 8

Injuries, Accidents and Laughs

"My God!" said the young reporter. "Will she ever dance again?" He had just read a review of mine in which I had casually reported that there had been, the night before, a last-minute cast change because so-and-so was out with a torn ligament. When writing my report, I had thought nothing of the incident except for a fleeting "too bad," because there are hazards to dancing, or to any extreme exercise, and accidents are inevitable.

The shocked attitude of my reporter colleague, about what I considered to be a run-of-the-mill accident, caused me to query others not associated with dancing. I found that they too would feel that report of a dancer having a broken bone, a torn ligament, a pulled tendon, a ripped muscle would be almost tantamount to reporting the end of a career. Dancers, if I may use the expression, take such injuries in their stride. They are impatient to get back to work and, if anything, they are irritated with themselves for permitting an injury to take place. Usually, it *is* the fault of the dancer, for the majority of injuries come from carelessness; a few, from accidents outside the dancer's control.

The most common cause of dance injuries is failure of the dancer to warm up his body sufficiently before going onstage or before practicing leaps, jumps or other movements which require easy elasticity of the body. In rehearsal and in class, most dancers wear, over their basic tights, woolen "leg-warmers," which vary in length according to the desires of the individual, or they may simply wear heavy woolen tights. At the start of a rehearsal, the dancer may also find need for a snug, small lightweight sweater which is removed as soon as the body is warm.

But warming from the outside is not enough. The dancer must warm his body from the inside out. He does this by starting out with easy stretches, limberings of all sorts—some dancers use modern dance floor stretches, others employ yoga exercises, the average dancer simply works out a series of warm-up exercises most beneficial to him. After this, there is customarily a barre workout, before rehearsal or perform- ance, just as there is in the classroom itself.

A class, however, is a continuous activity, whether it is the standard one and one-half hours, or a one-hour class for pointe work, adagio or some concentrated aspect of dance instruction, or the brief period before a performance; and once the dancer is warmed up, he stays warm. Not so at re- hearsal, and here the dancer must watch out. He may have had his warm-up, then rehearsed a ballet or a section of a ballet and then found himself temporarily unneeded for an hour, more or less—just time enough to get cool and, perhaps, a little stiff. From this otherwise welcome respite, he will be called to dance "full out" for the next part of his rehearsal.

He will have retained, of course, much of the limberness achieved during his formal warm-up, but if he has been sitting on the floor or a bench, he'll need to bend his knees, kick a leg lightly, twist the torso, perhaps touch his toes, or whatever he wishes, in the minute between his call back to rehearsal and getting to his place.

Daily classes, rehearsals and performances govern the regimen which a dancer must follow in his daily life. It is a hard life physically, but a healthy one, for the body—organs as well as muscles—is toned to perfection. Neither rust nor waste is permitted to erode the dancer's only instrument, his body. The dancer, then, achieves through his training as near perfect a body as a human can get.

But the life of the dancer can, at times, see strain make do for strength. This is rarely the individual dancer's fault, except for the overeager one who takes too many classes a day, goes on foolish diets, gets insufficient rest and places unnecessary demands on a weary body; but the demands of a career can sometime stretch endurance from strength to strain.

Rehearsals for a repertory season or a tour test the stamina of any dancer. A corps de ballet performer may have to learn anywhere from twenty to thirty different ballets or, if a veteran, at least rehearse the same ballets for the benefit of newcomers in an ever changing personnel. The hours are long and the task arduous but worth every ache to the dedicated dancer. The body, however, can rebel, and it usually gives fair warning. It does this not through the ordinary aches which dancers live with all their lives (if one muscle isn't sore, another one will be), but through an extra, unfamiliar discomfort or pain or, perhaps, swelling. This means that something is approaching the breaking point and insists upon a rest, and if the dancer doesn't respond, the tormented muscle or tendon is going to cause an enforced rest.

Tearing, or actually breaking, the achilles tendon is one of the worst dancing injuries. The non-dancer, if such an accident happened to him, would probably assume that he would be partly incapacitated for life. Not the dancer. He'll dance again. But in most instances, he had had the warning before the injury. Every dancer that I have talked to who ever suffered such a break has told me that the tendon had been sore in class, in rehearsal or in performance, not just fleetingly from a sharp pull, but steadily, naggingly. The warning was there; it wasn't heeded.

I remember attending a modern dance program by José Limón and his company in which the brilliant Pauline Koner was guest artist. Partway through a trio, there was a loud sound, rather like a pistol report, and Miss Koner hopped to the wings with a completely broken achilles tendon which one could see rolling up the back of her leg under the skin. She was rushed to a hospital and operated on immediately, before the tendon could begin to atrophy, but her attending doctor, who was not a "dance" doctor (oh, yes, there are doctors who know that dancers are unlike mere mortals), said she would be two years away from the stage. In six months, she was practicing; in nine months, she was dancing on stage. The scar tissue built up around the tear forecasts that she'll never break *that* tendon again; maybe another one somewhere. Incidentally, when Miss Koner returned to dancing, she quite naturally favored the recuperating leg, and by placing extra burdens on the other, she wound up with bruised and painful metatarsal arches which took some seasons to cure.

But Miss Koner herself told me that she had had her warning, that for the last rehearsal sessions before the Limón concert, the achilles had been very uncomfortable. She ignored it; and she paid for it. Other dancers have done the same.

The knee, which is very possibly the most complex and yet the weakest joint in the body, is subject to all kinds of injuries. Dancers are more careful of it than of any other part. Knee operations, from New York to Copenhagen and back, seem to be the inevitable answers to an occupational hazard.

After long bus rides, with the dancers traveling for hours in cramped positions, extra-careful warm-ups are necessary before rehearsal or performance. Sometimes a dancer can injure a knee just by being . . . well, a dancer. I know of a highly skillful technician who headed her own company of dancers. Reading in bed one night, with her legs crossed underneath her, one of the limbs fell asleep. Most of us have experienced the numbness and prickles which go with a leg or arm which has "gone to sleep" because of body weight pressed unduly upon it. Most of us would just unfold, unwind or, perhaps, stand up, until circulation returned to normal. Not this dancer, She hopped out of bed and, to wake up the offending member, started to toss off a batch of bent-knee leg swings to the front, side and back. There was a nasty stab of pain even in a numb leg which she really couldn't control, and cartilages slipped about. Next day? A knee operation.

So it is that most dancers, being careful instead of importunate, heeding nature's warnings instead of charging wildly ahead, can avoid most self-inflicted injuries. What cannot be avoided, in all instances, are injuries which may come from slippery or badly pitted stages, exposed nails, costumes and props difficult to maneuver, broken glass and, of course, fire.

It was fire which destroyed the career and the life of a teen-age dancer, Emma Livry, protegée of the immortal Taglioni. Her dress caught fire on the gas-illuminated stage, and the promise of a great talent was never fulfilled.

A tricky costume can also cause trouble. A train, a scarf, an extra length of skirt can mean a trip and a fall. A male dancer I knew lifted his besequined partner onto his shoulder and her brilliants scraped his neck; on the second lift, a fingernail got caught, and he broke his thumb.

In Gerald Arpino's striking ballet *Ropes,* the male dancers, called upon to hang upside down or in rope-supported aerial patterns rather like circus acrobats, in one scene use the ropes to elevate and frame in space the ballet's only female figure. And accidents will happen—once, the rope holding the girl failed to rise and she had to improvise something on the floor; but on another occasion, she rose, the ropes got entangled and she came close to being badly bruised, if not strangled.

In the famous ballet-centered movie of the 1930's, *Ballerina,* one of the first major films to be devoted to a ballet theme, behind-the-scenes jealousy led to the loosening of a trapdoor, the plummeting accident of the dancer and the crippling which followed.

Accidents caused by malevolence can also happen off-screen. Irina Baronova, cast in the title role of *Firebird* in New York, made her dazzling entrance and both shoulder straps of her costume broke and the bodice fell. The threads had been cut just to the degree that any port de bras would tear them loose. Another ballerina, slated to dance Black

Swan one night, put on her toe shoes early, in order to break them in, and discovered that ground glass had been secreted in the tip. These evildoings occurred in America, but they were engineered by Continental minds (as in *Ballerina*), where recourse to "planned" accidents had been predictable since the days of Camargo. Such happenings faded away as foreign dancers adjusted themselves to American ways and as Americans took over the duties of ballet in America.

Not that American dancers were not subject also to jealousies and to the inexorable pushing of a career. But they went about it differently. They would backbite, connive, cajole, lie and, perhaps, even bribe, but slashed costumes, ground glass in slippers, falling sandbags and unsecured trapdoors belonged to the Old World.

Stage surfaces are not often ideal, partly because they were not constructed with dancers in mind and partly because they have become pitted, gouged and splintered by supports, screwed into the floor, for theatrical sets. When a ballet troupe goes on the road, it expects to meet with all kinds of faulty stages. Today, the major companies actually carry with them their own floor; it is thin and compact and familiar to the dancers, but even this floor, providing a surface of the right texture, cannot eliminate a raked stage, that is, a stage which slopes downward toward the orchestra (a common design in Europe's old theaters), and the dancers have to make their own adjustments.

But theaters on the road should not be expected to take full blame for bad stage surfaces. The old Metropolitan Opera House in New York City had a notoriously bad stage surface (in between repair periods). Fortunately, it wasn't waxed, as so many so-called provincial stages are (they look

pretty, the wood is protected, but they are lethal to dancers),
but it had lots of holes in it. On one occasion, the ballet was
William Dollar's *Constantia*, there was an accident in that
passage when two men slide a girl, her forward foot outstretched and touching the floor, across the stage. Her foot
caught in a hole and she suffered a broken toe.

After a brilliant performance of the Black Swan by Nora
Kaye at the old Met, I asked her if she had any special secret
for executing the thirty-two fouettés without traveling one
inch from where she started. Her answer, "Self-preservation.
When you walk to stage center you glance down casually
and pick the one place without holes in it and you stay there,
or it's good-night Charlie!"

The Bolshoi Ballet from Moscow, when it first visited New
York, flatly refused to dance on the Met stage until some
basic repairs had been made. And the Royal Danish Ballet,
traveling with what is called a ground-cloth—a stage-size
piece of material which provides good texture for dancing
but which is only as flat as the boards it covers—decided it
was safer to dance on the bare stage. "At least you could see
the hazards," said one, "and try to avoid them. But with the
ground-cloth, you might think you're stepping on a flat surface and then lose your toe in a hidden hole."

Some new stages, such as Lincoln Center's New York State
Theater, have stage surfaces of linoleum-like modern material over the wooden floor, but if wooden floors provide the
actual surface, dancers prefer floorboards made of hard wood
—and lying not on cement but on supports which provide
air-space for resiliency, and with no varnish or wax used.
Ted Shawn, veteran of theater experiences around the world,
and director of the first theater in America especially built

for dance at the Jacob's Pillow Dance Festival, recommends old-fashioned tongue oil as a preservative for the wood, but a treatment which will not make the surface slick (however, tongue oil must soak in, and it takes several months for the process to work properly).

Still, dancers meet with slippery stages. Sometimes an un-waxed, unvarnished stage can be slippery simply because it was washed with soap (only water and, if necessary, some lye should be used to clean the surface), but slippery for whatever reason, dancers must cope with it. The most com-mon corrective is rosin, and the rosin box in the wings of a ballet theater is a trademark of the profession. The box usu-ally has rosin crystals, or chunks (although there is a less satisfactory rosin powder), and the dancers step in, one foot at a time, and grind the rosin, which contains adhesive qual-ities, into the pointe of the toe shoe or onto the soles of the slippers. Both men and women use it for stage, rehearsal studio or classroom. And it is used before every entrance throughout a ballet.

Sometimes, a stage can be so skiddy that even rosin slides about on it. Dancers have all sorts of semi-cures for such. Pouring Coca-Cola on the floor and stepping into it gives the soles of the shoes a temporary stickiness which helps to re-buff a slick floor. Gritty kitchen cleansers also help. And extra protection can be obtained by gluing rubber soles onto the dancing shoes. Toe shoes which are darned are less likely to skid than those with untouched, smooth, satin pointes.

If the indispensable rosin box is part of any backstage scene at the ballet, the watering can is a nostalgic reminder of the days when teachers of ballet sprinkled the floor of the studio (and sometimes obstreperous young charges!) with water by way of inducing a grip-ingredient between the dancer's foot and the boards themselves.

Not all of the hazards to which the dancer's body (or poise) is subject are necessarily serious. Some of the accidents which occur on stage are actually funny and have given rise to an endless and delightful series of anecdotes, not about "The Perils of Pauline," but rather "The Perils of Performing." Let me recount a few.

There is a difficult and physically brilliant passage in *Serenade,* in which the danseur, with legs spread and arms at ready for the catch, stands slightly to the left (stage left, that is) of center stage. The female dancer, starting from the downstage wings at stage right, runs on the diagonal line across the stage and, just before she reaches him, does a grand jeté with the right leg aimed to go under the danseur's right arm, but in a split second, she reverses her body direction in midair and the catch is made with the right leg now to the rear of the girl's body and the body itself facing the direction from which she came. It is a striking bit of virtuosity and it almost always receives a round of applause. But at one performance on tour there was a slippery stage to increase the perils of this passage. The male dancer stood in position, and Maria Tallchief, who was dancing that section, ran out from the wings stage right, slipped, and then slid in a sitdown position directly through her partner's legs and into the wings stage left. With aplomb and becoming gallantry, the male dancer, with arms outstretched, followed her course, and as she shot through his legs, made a most elegant sweep toward her and then turned with arms outstretched in the direction along which she had departed as if, in gesture, he had said, "Here she comes and . . . there she goes!"

Alicia Markova, tiny and fragile-looking, light and airy and as dainty as a Taglioni lithograph, tells of the time she was dancing on an outdoor platform and tripped over a loose board. Sometimes, the ballerina can recover her balance or, perhaps, sink to the floor gracefully, but Markova was falling straight front and, as she says, "making a rapid descent in clouds of tulle directly onto my stomach. I tried desperately in those seconds to recall some sweet pose of a Romantic Age ballerina captured in a lithograph. I couldn't. I just went flat."

Dame Alicia, however, could recoup from unexpected accidents as only a real pro can do. Toward the end of her dancing career, she was performing in her greatest triumph, *Giselle*. In Act I, there is a sequence in which she hops on one pointe diagonally across the stage. At a given performance at the old Metropolitan Opera House in New York, the great ballerina did two hops and then, apparently, fell off pointe (a hole, a ridge, an unevenness in the stage floor could cause it to happen to any dancer), and the audience gasped. Unperturbed, the ballerina created a new pattern—two hops on pointe, one off pointe. The audience sighed happily; they knew that they must have seen Markova's version of this variation. A lesser performer would simply have hoisted herself back up and continued on pointe, thus making it clear that an error had occurred. Markova translated an unintentional error into a choreographic pattern.

Markova not only refused to show errors (except for the unadaptable fall) but also refused to show effort, and this led many times to some near-accidents on stage. The ballet world knew that the tiny star was difficult to partner, especially with lifts, because in her determination to show effortlessness, she would simply stand there and let the male lift her absolutely deadweight. When she danced in the Metropolitan Opera's production of Gluck's *Orfeo ed Euridice,* an exceptionally muscular male dancer—he had been a boxer—was assigned to lift Markova in certain passages. In rehearsal, he could barely get her off the floor, let alone high in space, despite her weight of only ninety-five pounds. Embarrassed, he said, "Madame, I must be doing something wrong." Markova smiled her sweetest smile and replied, "It will be all right in performance."

The young man naturally assumed that the ballerina had been merely "marking" (walking through) the movements and that in performance she would take a breath, do a plié and push herself upward. Came performance time, the biceps boy was all ready for the lightest of ballerinas to give her partner some help on the lifts. But no. The time came, and she merely stood prettily. Sheer male vanity made him raise this tiny creature, who looked like fluff and stood like lead, over his head, as muscles and veins bulged in protest. As his tormented arms slowly let her down to the ground, she turned to him and said, ever so sweetly in her most ladylike tea-and-scones voice, "You see?"

Nora Kaye had some funny accidents happen during the most serious scenes of intense dance drama. In Valerie Bettis's dance version of the Tennessee Williams play *A Streetcar Named Desire,* there is a scene in which Blanche is about to be ravished by Stanley and puts up a terrified protest (although she has really invited such a course of action). At one performance, Kaye, her fists clenched and held high, was doing violent turns, and Igor Youskevitch (as Stanley) stepped in, a fraction too soon, to grab her and was hit on the temple by a Kaye fist and knocked out cold.

Improvising, the ballerina did an erotic and intensely dynamic dance over the inert body. "What else could I do?" she asked after the performance. "Short of lying down and pulling Igor on top of me, I couldn't think of any other way to finish the scene." When she arrived at an elegant supper party after the performance and was formally announced, she said to her host and hostess, "Oh, just call me Butch Kaye."

But my very favorite Kaye story of all, which I have told and retold in print and in lectures, has to do with a wildly funny contretemps in the ballet which made Nora Kaye a star, Antony Tudor's *Pillar of Fire.*

Most ballet fans will remember that, in *Pillar,* the central figure, Hagar, is a frustrated virgin who finds herself growing up to be like her prim elder sister and losing potential beaux, or so she thinks, to her coquettish younger sister. There is one man she loves but she is led to believe, mistakenly, that he cares for the younger girl. Hence, in a moment of desperation and defiance, she leaves her own proper home and enters a mysterious, tortured house where revels are held, across the way. And she gives herself to a sullen, sexy libertine.

The anecdote concerns an ensuing scene in which Hagar, remorseful and ashamed, leaps onto the stage as if she would escape her own sin, and is lifted high, in horizontal position, by a chorus of three men. One holds her close to the shoulders, another by one leg, and the third boy controls Hagar's extended leg, so that the ballerina actually does a pirouette,

with leg extended in front of the body, lying flat in air instead of being vertical on the ground. It is an exciting moment and dramatically pertinent to Hagar's emotional state.

At one performance at the old Met, just before Kaye's entrance with the grand jetés, Ruth Ann Koesun, who was
playing the Younger Sister, got a charleyhorse—cramps in
the calf of the leg—onstage. She hopped to the wings on her
working leg and proceeded to lie down while her husband,
one of the three men scheduled to lift Miss Kaye, started to
massage her cramped leg. The second of the three men stood
by Miss Koesun out of concern for her temporary indisposi-
tion. The third male, hearing the musical cue, got onstage,
took a wide stance and opened his arms, knowing perfectly
well that he could not lift the ballerina by her head, by a foot
and generate the turn in the middle. But there he was, a
stalwart American youth ready to do his best.

As Ralph McWilliams stood there, prepared to do whatever Miss Kaye might indicate, the ballerina leaped onto
stage, sized up the situation, and improvised a continuation
of the jetés around the stage. As she flew by the lone male,
she murmured through unmoving lips, "Where the hell is
everybody!"

The theater of the mid and latter half of the twentieth
century might well echo that query. And the answer would
be that almost everybody now goes to the ballet as well as
to opera, drama and musicals. What had been, earlier in the
century, a performing art that seemed too esoteric for the
average theatergoer, and had gone through a period of hiber-
nation in which it was barely tolerated in royal and state
theaters and in opera houses as a minor and not very popular

adjunct to grand opera, found itself reborn as one of the major creative forces of the century and as one of the biggest box office attractions in theater history.

Ballet, once the plaything of Catherine de Medici and her courtiers, had branched out into every city and almost every town of any size in the United States. It successfully invaded the legitimate theaters of Broadway and the great new art centers springing up all over the nation. It found outlets in the musical theater, on television and even as an educational force in schools and colleges. It came to be used, along with other forms of dance, as an instrument of therapy for curing the ills of both body and mind.

Ballet, indeed, without rejecting its royal and aristocratic academic origins, had emerged as an exhilarating and friendly companion to the dance-going peoples of the world.

Glossary

ADAGIO   A dance in slow tempo. Also, that portion of a classical *pas de deux* in which the ballerina, assisted by her partner, displays her beauty of line and her mastery of flowing, lyrical, and sustained movements.

ALLEGRO   A dance sequence in fast tempo.

ARABESQUE   A traditional ballet position in which the dancer stands on one leg with the other leg extended behind in a straight line. Positions of the arms may vary and the distance between the free leg and the floor may also vary. In an *arabesque penché*, for example, the body is tilted forward and the free leg extends high into space, sometimes reaching a position vertical to the floor. (See illustrations and cover photograph.)

ATTITUDE   A traditional ballet position in which the dancer stands on one leg with the other leg raised behind the body but with bent knee. The pose was inspired by Bologna's famed statue of the god Mercury. If the free leg is extended to the front, instead of to the rear, and adheres to the same spatial design as the movement described above, it may also be referred to as an *attitude*. (See illustrations.)

BALLERINA   The term is misused when applied to any female dancer. The *ballerina* is a leading female dancer in a ballet company and if a major company has two or more *ballerinas* on its roster of stars, the principal one may be called a *prima ballerina*. The highest rank, given to the greatest female dancer of a nation and of an era, is *prima ballerina assoluta,* last officially awarded by the Czar of Russia to Mathilde Kchessinskaya (or Kchessinska).

BALLET   Derived from the Italian word *ballare,* meaning "to dance."

BALLET D'ACTION   A ballet with a story.

BALLETOMANE   A person devoted to the ballet, a fan, who attends as many performances as possible, is an appreciative and critical viewer, and strives to interest others in the art.

BALLON   A term applicable to the execution of all dance movements in air. The resilience of the dancer and his ability to rise easily off the ground in a jump or leap and to descend lightly.

BATTEMENT   A kick, either high (*grand battement*) or low. In a *battement tendu,* the kick extends only as far as the stretched foot will allow with the tip of the toe remaining on the floor. It may be done in any direction. (See illustrations.)

BATTERIE   The term applied to all movements in which the legs and feet beat together, usually in air (*entrechat, brisé, cabriole,* etc.). In the classroom, certain preparatory exercises involving beats are done at the ballet *barre.* The dancer stands on one foot while the free foot accomplishes the beats.

BOURRÉE   See PAS DE BOURRÉE.

BRISÉ   A leg-beat in air. The dancer rises from the floor, beats one leg against the other and lands on both feet in *fifth position.* A *brisé* varies from the *entrechat* in that only one leg does the beating movement, and it varies from the *cabriole* in that the landing is made on both feet.

CABRIOLE   A virtuosic movement in air (usually for male dancers but not exclusively) in which one leg swings out in a high kick and is held at the peak of its extension while the other leg leaves the floor and strikes it in a swift beat or beats. The legs are straight, the feet pointed, and the movement may be done to the front, rear, or side. (See *Brisé.*)

CARACTÈRE   A term used to describe a dancer who performs non-classical character or national dances—such as a czardas or gypsy dance—in a ballet. A *demi-caractère* dancer is one who is called upon to combine character steps with classical action.

CHANGEMENT DE PIEDS   A step in which the dancer jumps from *fifth position,* changes the feet in air and lands in *fifth position* but with the position of the feet reversed (if the dancer starts with the right leg in front, he will finish with the right leg in back).

CHOREOGRAPHER   The creator of a ballet, the one who invents, selects, and designs the steps and the movements and puts them into rhythmic, geometric, or dramatic sequences which have form, progression, and purpose.

CODA The concluding portion of a *pas de deux* or ballet.

CORPS DE BALLET The chorus or ensemble of a ballet company.

CORYPHÉE A dancing rank which lies between *corps de ballet* dancer and soloist. One who is assigned a few phrases of movement distinct from the actions of the *corps* but who does not perform a complete solo.

DANSE D'ÉCOLE The classic dance, the dance based upon the traditional technique of the classical ballet.

DANSEUR NOBLE A classical male dancer, independent soloist, and partner to the *ballerina*.

DÉVELOPPÉ The gradual unfolding of the leg as it is raised in an extension from the floor. Performed to the front, back, or side. The unfolding action is centered in the knee, which bends as the working leg is withdrawn from the floor and which is straightened when the peak of the extension is achieved.

DIVERTISSEMENT A dance or a series of danced episodes without plot. An entire ballet may be a *divertissement* or the term may apply to the "diverting" interludes in a dramatic ballet.

ÉCHAPPÉ A step in which the dancer's feet move swiftly from a "closed" to "open" position and from soles flat on the floor to *demi-pointe* or, in the case of the female dancer, full *pointe*. Executed from *first* or *fifth positions* to *second position*, either with a jump or with a quick *relevé*.

ELEVATION Aerial action, the ability of the dancer to move as easily in air as on the ground (related to *ballon*).

EN ARRIÈRE To the back.

EN AVANT To the front.

EN DEDANS Inward (toward the body).

EN DEHORS Outward (away from the body).

ENTRECHAT A vertical jump, with the body held in a plumb line, during which the dancer changes the position of his feet several times with a beating of the legs. The number of changes achieved indicate an *entrechat quatre, entrechat six,* etc. (See illustrations.)

ENTRÉE An entrance, such as the opening passages of a *grand pas de deux* or a suite of dances.

FIVE POSITIONS The traditional positions of the feet (there are related and numbered positions of the arms also) in ballet. (See illustrations.)

FOUETTÉ A whipping movement of the working leg which propels the dancer into a turn, into multiple turns, or shifts of direction.

GARGOUILLADE A movement in air (closely related to the *pas de chat*) in which the knees are drawn up equally high at the climax of the leap while the leading foot describes a circle in space *en dehors* and the other foot moves through a circle *en dedans.* In a loose play on words, dancers sometimes refer to it as "gargling with the feet."

GLISSADE   A smooth, gliding movement starting from *fifth position,* separating into an open-leg position (rather like a leap held to the floor), and returning to *fifth position.*

JETÉ   A leap in which the dancer pushes off the floor with one leg, describes an arc in air, and lands on the other foot. In a *grand jeté,* the dancer seeks the highest elevation possible to him, with the leading leg thrusting out and up as high as the body structure will permit and the propelling leg, once it has left the floor, reaching back to a high extension. Sometimes a near-split may be achieved in a *grand jeté.* (See illustrations.)

LIBRETTO   The story of a ballet or the plot, incident, or theme on which it is based.

MODERN DANCE   A free dance developed concurrently in America and in Central Europe during the twentieth century. Unlike ballet, it has no traditional vocabulary of movement from which dancers and choreographers may draw standard steps. It possesses highly advanced technical skills and methods for classroom training but the dances themselves are composed of freshly invented actions inspired by the music, idea, period, and purpose of the piece.

NOTATION   A script method for writing down the movements of a dance or ballet so they may be revived or reproduced by others capable of reading the script. Methods employing stick figures, sometimes placed on a musical staff and in other cases paired with musical symbols, have been used for several centuries. The most exact form of notation known today is called *Labanotation.* Another contemporary notational method, developed in England, is the *Benesh system.*

PANTOMIME   Imitative movement, usually gestural, by which emotions, character, and the key points in a plot are communicated to an audience. Both realistic and stylized gesture may be used. Among the traditional gestures used in ballet, those indicating Love (the hands are pressed against the heart), or Anger (arms are raised above the head and fists are shaken), may be considered reasonably realistic while Dance (hands circling around each other over the head), and Queen (the index finger touches either side of the brow where a crown might rest), would be looked upon as stylized gestures.

PAS   A danced step or movement. Also used to denote a short dance or dance passage (in this sense, usually used with a modifier, such as *pas seul* or *pas de deux,* etc.).

PAS D'ACTION   Episodes in ballet which advance the plot, introduce dramatic incident, or establish relationships among the characters. A combination of dancing and pantomime.

PAS DE BASQUE   A light, sliding step (name derives from Basque dancing).

PAS DE BOURRÉE   A walking step, usually swift, done on the ball of the foot or, with the female dancer, usually on *pointe*. The dancer may travel in any direction and the steps are customarily so short that the separation between the dancer's legs as she moves is barely discernible.

PAS DE CHAT   A catlike step. From a *plié* in *fifth position,* the dancer leaps into the air, drawing up one leg (with bent knee) and immediately duplicating the action with the other leg so that at the peak of elevation, the toes almost meet in air.

PAS DE DEUX   A dance for two. A classical *grand pas de deux* is performed by a *ballerina* and a *premier danseur* and is divided into an *entrée, adagio,* two *variations,* and *coda.* Also, *pas de trois* (a dance for three), *pas de quatre* (for four), *pas de cinq* (for five), *pas de six* (for six), etc.

PAS DE POISSON   A climactic movement in a phrase of action in which the female dancer hurls herself in the direction of the floor and is caught by her partner as her body bends upward in a fishlike arc. When the male dancer jumps upward and describes a similar arc of the body, the movement may also be described as a *pas de poisson,* although this male movement is actually a form of *soubresaut.* The same body line is described in space at the peak of a *cabriole en arrière.* (See illustrations.)

PIROUETTE   A turn of the body on one foot. Usually, the female does the movement on *pointe;* the male, always on *demi-pointe* (on the ball of the foot). The free leg may be held in any of a number of approved positions—against the ankle of the working leg or higher up along the calf, straight out to the side (*à la seconde, en attitude,* etc.). (See illustrations.)

PLIÉ   A bending of the knees, with the hips, legs, and feet turned outward. A *demi-plié* is a small knee-bend while a *grand-plié* is a deep knee-bend. This is the movement which enables the dancer to spring high into the air and to return to the ground (when a second *plié* is done) lightly, without jarring.

POINTE   The tip of the toe. The female dancer, when she is dancing *sur les pointes* (or, more popularly, on *pointe*) is moving on the tips of her toes and wearing blocked toe slippers which give her added support. Toe dancing, incidentally, is not synonymous with the word *ballet,* for ballet existed long before the *ballerina* rose onto *pointe* and long before the toe slipper was invented. *Pointe* dancing added new physical peril, new movement possibilities, and new beauty to the basic, established technique of ballet.

PORT DE BRAS   The positions and the movements of the arms. (See illustrations.)

RELEVÉ   Rising onto *pointe* or *demi-pointe*.

RÉVÉRENCE   A low, courtly, graceful bow.

ROND DE JAMBE   A rotary movement of the leg either on the floor or in the air (*à terre* or *en l'air*).

SAUTÉ   A jump.

TERRE-À-TERRE   Steps which are done on the ground.

TIGHTS   The skin-tight garment which encases the body from trunk to feet.

TOUR   A turn. A *pirouette* is a *tour* but the term is usually employed with a modifier, such as *tour jeté, tour en l'air,* etc.

TOUR EN L'AIR   One of the most brilliant movements for the male dancer (although it is sometimes executed by the female). From *fifth position* in *demi-plié*, the dancer springs straight up into the air and does a complete turn of the body before landing in the position from which he started. Most male dancers can accomplish a double turn in air, a few can do triples. In a virtuosic sequence, the male dancer may be called upon to execute a whole series of doubles, one right after the other.

TURNOUT   The body position characteristic of ballet, with the legs turned out from the hips at (with professional dancers and advanced students but *not* beginners) a 180-degree angle.

TUTU   The skirt worn by the female ballet dancer. In the romantic style (instituted by Taglioni), it reached almost to the ankle. In the later classic style it has been shortened so the entire leg is revealed, the *tutu* extending out from the hips rather like a huge powder puff.

VARIATION   A solo dance. The same as *pas seul*.

Appendix: List of Ballets

The Afternoon of a Faun (L'Après-midi d'un Faune)
Choreography: Vaslav Nijinsky; music: Claude Debussy; scenery and costumes: Léon Bakst. First produced by Diaghileff's Ballet Russes, Paris, May 29, 1912. First American performance, same company, New York, Jan. 18, 1916. Entirely new conception and production with choreography by Jerome Robbins, music of Debussy, costumes by Irene Sharaff, décor and lighting by Jean Rosenthal. First performance, New York, May 14, 1953, New York City Ballet. Also produced by Jerome Robbins' Ballets: U.S.A. Other less successful versions have been done since the Nijinsky original was first produced.

The Age of Anxiety
Choreography: Jerome Robbins; music: Leonard Bernstein (Second Symphony, based upon the poem, "The Age of Anxiety" by W. H. Auden); scenery: Oliver Smith; costumes: Irene Sharaff. First produced by the New York City Ballet, New York, Feb. 26, 1950.

Agon
Choreography: George Balanchine; music: Igor Stravinsky. First presented by the New York City Ballet, New York, in a benefit preview Nov. 27, 1957, and with the formal première taking place Dec. 1. Among other versions the most prominent is that with choreography by Kenneth MacMillan, music of Stravinsky, scenery and costumes by Nicholas Georgiadis. First performance, London, Aug. 20, 1958, Royal Ballet.

Aleko

Choreography: Leonide Massine; music: Tchaikovsky (Trio in A Minor, orchestrated by Erno Rapée); book: Massine and Chagall, based on the Pushkin poem "Gypsies"; scenery and costumes: Marc Chagall. First produced by Ballet Theatre (now American Ballet Theatre), Mexico City, summer 1942. First New York performance, Oct. 6, 1942.

Allegro Brillante

Choreography: George Balanchine; music: Tchaikovsky (single movement of the unfinished Third Piano Concerto). First produced by the New York City Ballet, New York, Mar. 1, 1956.

L'Amour et Son Amour (Cupid and His Love)

Choreography: Jean Babilée; music: César Franck (Psyché); scenery and costumes: Jean Cocteau. First produced by Les Ballets des Champs-Élysées, Paris, Dec. 13, 1948. First American performance by Ballet Theatre (now American Ballet Theatre), Apr. 17, 1951.

Apollo (Apollon Musagète)

Choreography: George Balanchine; music and book: Igor Stravinsky; scenery and costumes: André Bauchant. First presented by Diaghileff's Ballets Russes, Paris, June 12, 1928. First American performance by the American Ballet, New York, Apr. 27, 1937, with scenery and costumes by Stewart Chaney. Also added to the repertories of Ballet Theatre (now American Ballet Theatre), Apr. 25, 1943, the New York City Ballet, Nov. 15, 1951, the San Francisco Ballet and other companies in Europe (including the Royal Ballet, London, and the Royal Danish Ballet) and South America. The Stravinsky score had been commissioned by Elizabeth Sprague Coolidge and had had its first presentation at the Library of Congress on Apr. 27, 1928, in a staging (no longer used) by Adolph Bolm. Immediately after this Washington première, the composer turned his work over to Diaghileff and Balanchine.

Aurora's Wedding (Also, *Princess Aurora*) (See *The Sleeping Beauty*)

Aurora's Wedding or, as it is called in the American Ballet Theatre production, *Princess Aurora*, is actually the final act of the three-act *The Sleeping Beauty*, choreographed by Marius Petipa, with music by Tchaikovsky. Since the concluding act is composed mainly of *divertissements*, it is frequently produced as an independent short ballet. It contains the famous *Bluebird Pas de Deux* and the *Grand Pas de Deux* for Aurora and her cavalier, as well as national dances, character dances, and the like. Adaptations, deletions, and additions have been made by choreographers engaged to restage the work as a complete ballet. Because of its glittering background and costumes, its virtuosic classical dances, and its variety of shorter numbers, *Aurora's Wedding* has long enjoyed an enormously popular career separate from the mother creation, *The Sleeping Beauty*. It was presented as a one-act production by the Diaghileff Ballets Russes, May 18, 1922, and is active in the repertories of the Ballet Russe de Monte Carlo, the American Ballet Theatre, the Paris Opera Ballet, and other companies.

Bacchanale
Choreography: Leonide Massine; music: Richard Wagner *(Tannhäuser)*; libretto, scenery, costumes: Salvador Dali. First produced by the Ballet Russe de Monte Carlo, New York, Nov. 9, 1939.

Le Baiser de la Fée (The Fairy's Kiss)
Choreography: George Balanchine; music and book: Igor Stravinsky; scenery and costumes: Alicia Halicka. First produced by the American Ballet, Apr. 27, 1937, New York. Presented by the Ballet Russe de Monte Carlo, Apr. 10, 1940, New York. Revived, New York City Ballet, Nov. 28, 1950, New York. Earlier presentations took place abroad, and among them was a version choreographed by Frederick Ashton for the Sadler's Wells Ballet (now the Royal Ballet). Among notable recent productions is that with choreography by Kenneth MacMillan, music by Stravinsky, scenery and costumes by Kenneth Rowell. Presented by the Royal Ballet, Apr. 12, 1960, London.

Ballet Imperial
Choreography: George Balanchine; music: Tchaikovsky (Piano Concerto No. 2); scenery and costumes: Mstislav Doboujinsky. First produced by the American Ballet, New York, May 27, 1941. Presented by the Ballet Russe de Monte Carlo in Chicago, 1944; New York, Feb. 20, 1945. Also staged for the Sadler's Wells Ballet (now the Royal Ballet), London, Apr. 5, 1950, with new scenery and costumes by Eugene Berman; revived for the Royal Ballet, London, Oct. 18, 1963, with scenery and costumes by Carl Toms. Staged for the New York City Ballet, New York, Oct. 15, 1964, with décor by Rouben Ter-Arutunian and costumes by Karinska. Other productions elsewhere.

La Bayadère (also *Bayaderka*)
Choreography: Marius Petipa; music: Leon Minkus; books: S. N. Khudekov. First presented by the Russian Imperial Ballet, St. Petersburg, Jan. 23 (Julian or Russian calendar), Feb. 4 (Gregorian or Western calendar), 1877. Act IV (The Kingdom of the Shades) was first presented in America by the Leningrad Kirov Ballet, Sept. 14, 1961. Restaged by Rudolph Nureyev, with costumes by Philip Prowse, it was added to the repertory of the Royal Ballet, London,

Nov. 27, 1963; presented by the same company in America, New York, May 9, 1965.

Le Beau Danube
Choreography: Leonide Massine; music: Johann Strauss; scenery: V. and E. Polunin; costumes: Comte Etienne de Beaumont. First produced by the Ballet Russe de Monte Carlo at Monte Carlo, Apr. 15, 1933. An earlier version presented in Paris by Comte Etienne de Beaumont, 1924. First American performance by the Ballet Russe, New York, Dec. 22, 1933.

Beauty and the Beast
Choreography: John Cranko; music: Maurice Ravel (excerpts from Mother Goose Suite); scenery and costumes: Margaret Kaye. First produced by the Sadler's Wells Theatre Ballet, London, Dec. 20, 1949. First American performance, Denver, Nov. 14, 1951.

La Belle au Bois Dormant (See *The Sleeping Beauty*)

Les Biches
Choreography: Bronislava Nijinska; music: Francis Poulenc; scenery and costumes: Marie Laurencin. First produced by the Diaghileff Ballets Russes, Monte Carlo, Jan. 6, 1924. Revived by the Marquis de Cuevas' Grand Ballet, Nov. 17, 1947, and first presented in America by that company, New York, Nov. 13, 1950. Revived by the Royal Ballet, London, Dec. 2, 1964.

Billy the Kid
Choreography: Eugene Loring; music: Aaron Copland; book: Lincoln Kirstein; scenery and costumes: Jared French. First produced by the Ballet Caravan, Chicago, Oct. 16, 1938. Presented by Ballet Theatre (now the American Ballet Theatre), New York, Feb. 13, 1941.

Birthday Offering
Choreography: Frederick Ashton; music: Alexander Glazounov; costumes: André Levasseur. First produced by the Sadler's Wells Ballet (now the Royal Ballet), London, May 5, 1956. First presented in America by the same company, New York, Sept. 11, 1957.

Black Swan (See *Swan Lake*)
Black Swan is the popular name given to the *pas de deux* for Odile and the Prince in Act III of *Swan Lake*. It contains the famous sequence of thirty-two *fouettés* for the ballerina.

Bluebeard
Choreography and book: Michel Fokine; music: Jacques Offenbach; scenery and costumes: Marcel Vertès. First produced by Ballet Theatre (now the American Ballet Theatre), Mexico City, Oct. 27, 1941; New York première by same company, Nov. 12, 1941.

Bluebird Pas de Deux (See *The Sleeping Beauty*)

This *pas de deux,* popularly known as the *Bluebird,* is contained in the last act of *The Sleeping Beauty.* It is also a part of *Aurora's Wedding* (or *Princess Aurora*), the name given to the closing act of *The Sleeping Beauty* when it is presented as an independent, one-act *divertissement.* In turn, the *Bluebird Pas de Deux* is frequently given as a separate item on a program of other ballets.

Bolero

This popular musical work by Maurice Ravel has been given many different stagings and wholly different choreographies. It has been conceived as a solo work, a group work, and a mass spectacle. Some choreographers have held it close to the ethnic patterns of Spanish dance, while others have used it in a more balletic manner. Among the innumerable dance versions of Ravel's *Bolero* are those created for the following: Ida Rubinstein, Ballet Theatre (choreography by Argentinita), the Markova-Dolin Ballet, the Philadelphia Ballet, the Royal Danish Ballet, the Marquis de Cuevas' Grand Ballet, Radio City Music Hall.

Bourrée Fantasque

Choreography: George Balanchine; music: Emmanuel Chabrier; costumes: Karinska. First produced by the New York City Ballet, New York, Dec. 1, 1949. European productions include that of the Festival Ballet, London, Aug. 18, 1960.

La Boutique Fantasque

Choreography: Leonide Massine; music: Rossini, arranged and orchestrated by Ottorino Respighi; scenery and costumes: André Derain. First produced by the Diaghileff Ballets Russes, London, June 5, 1919. First presented in America by the Ballet Russe de Monte Carlo, New York, Mar. 20, 1935.

Brahms-Schoenberg Quartet

Choreography: George Balanchine; music: Johannes Brahms (First Piano Quartet in G minor, orchestrated by Arnold Schoenberg); scenery: Peter Harvey; costumes: Karinska. First produced by the New York City Ballet, New York, Apr. 21, 1966.

Bugaku

Choreography: George Balanchine; music: Toshiru Mayuzumi; scenery: David Hays; costumes: Karinska. First produced by the New York City Ballet, New York, Mar. 20, 1963.

The Cage

Choreography: Jerome Robbins; music: Igor Stravinsky (Concerto Grosso in D for Strings); décor and lighting: Jean Rosenthal; costumes: Ruth Sobotka. First produced by the New York City Ballet, New York, June 14, 1951.

Cakewalk

Choreography: Ruthanna Boris; music: Louis Gottschalk, adapted and orchestrated by Hershy Kay; scenery and costumes: John Drew. First produced by the New York City Ballet, New York, June 12, 1951. Revived with scenery and costumes by William Pitkin by the City Center Joffrey Ballet, Sept. 8, 1966.

Cappriccio Espagnol

Choreography: Leonide Massine; music: Rimsky-Korsakoff; scenery and costumes: Mariano Andreù; choreographic collaboration: Argentinita. First produced by the Ballet Russe de Monte Carlo at Monte Carlo, May 4, 1939. First American performance, New York, Oct. 27, 1939, same company.

Caprichos

Choreography: Herbert Ross; music: Béla Bartók; costumes: Helene Pons. The ballet is based upon the Spanish artist Goya's commentaries on his own series of etchings by the same name; and the Bartók music, played as originally written (not expanded for orchestral use) is his Contrasts for Piano, Clarinet and Violin. First produced by the Choreographers' Workshop, New York, Jan. 29, 1950. First presented by Ballet Theatre (now the American Ballet Theatre), New York, Apr. 26, 1950.

Card Game (Also *Card Party, Jeu de Cartes* and *Poker Game*)

Choreography: George Balanchine; music and book: Igor Stravinsky; associate on the book: M. Malaieff; scenery and costumes: Irene Sharaff. First produced by the American Ballet, New York, Apr. 27, 1937. Revived by the Ballet Russe de Monte Carlo (as *Poker Game*), New York, Oct. 14, 1940. Revived by the New York City Ballet, New York, Feb. 15, 1951. A European production was staged in 1945, with choreography by Janine Charrat, by the Ballets des Champs-Elysées.

Carmen

Choreography: Roland Petit; music: Georges Bizet; scenery and costumes: Antoni Clavé; based on the opera of the same name. First produced by Roland Petit's Ballets de Paris, London, Feb. 21, 1949. First presented in America by the same company, New York, Oct. 6, 1949.

Carnaval

Choreography and book: Michel Fokine; music: Robert Schumann (orchestration of Carnaval, suite for piano); scenery and costumes: Léon Bakst. First performed at a benefit in St. Petersburg by members of the Russian Imperial Ballet in 1910. First performed by the Diaghileff Ballets Russes in Paris, June 4, 1910; American première, by the same company, New York, Jan. 19, 1916. Later revived in

America by the Ballet Russe de Monte Carlo and Ballet Theatre (now the American Ballet Theatre), the former Mar. 16, 1934, the latter in 1940.

Casse Noisette (See *The Nutcracker*)

La Chatte

Choreography: George Balanchine; music: Henri Sauget; book: Boris Kochno based on one of Aesop's fables; scenery and costumes: Gabo and Pevsner. First produced by Diaghileff's Ballets Russes, Monte Carlo, Apr. 30, 1927.

Checkmate

Choreography: Ninette de Valois; music: Arthur Bliss; scenery and costumes: E. McKnight Kauffer. First produced by the Vic-Wells Ballet (later the Sadler's Wells Ballet and now the Royal Ballet), Paris, June 15, 1937; first London performance, Oct. 5, 1937; first American performance (same company), Nov. 2, 1949.

Chopin Concerto

Choreography: Bronislava Nijinska; music: Chopin; costumes: Alexander Ignatieff. First produced by the Ballet Russe de Monte Carlo, New York, Oct. 12, 1942. (An earlier version was presented in Paris in 1937.)

Chopiniana (See also *Les Sylphides*)

Choreography: Michel Fokine; music: Chopin, orchestrated by Glazounov. First produced in St. Petersburg, Mar. 8, 1908, by members of the Russian Imperial Ballet, with Anna Pavlova and Anatole Oboukhoff. (An earlier version, using the figure of Chopin, was presented in 1906; Russian, English, and American authorities and Fokine himself are not in agreement on the date of the first performance of the second version, although the year is most probably 1908 and the month February or March.) Later revised and renamed *Les Sylphides*, and with scenery and costumes by Alexandre Benois, it was presented by Diaghileff's Ballets Russes in Paris, June 2, 1909. Pavlova and Vaslav Nijinsky danced in the Paris première.

Choreartium

Choreography: Leonide Massine; music: Brahms (Symphony No. 4); scenery and costumes: Constantine Terechkovich and Eugene Lourie. First produced by the Ballet Russe de Monte Carlo, London, Oct. 24, 1933. First American presentation, New York, Oct. 16, 1935.

Cinderella

Choreography: Frederick Ashton; music: Serge Prokofieff; scenery and costumes: Jean-Denis Malclès. First produced by the Sadler's Wells Ballet (now the Royal Ballet), London, Dec. 23, 1948. First

American presentation by the same company, New York, Oct. 18, 1949. New production by the same company with scenery and costumes by Henry Bardon and David Walker, London, Dec. 23, 1965; first American presentation, New York, Apr. 18, 1967. Other stagings of *Cinderella* include the following: Soviet ballet, choreography: R. Zakharov; music: Prokofieff, Moscow, Nov. 21, 1945 (the Bolshoi Theatre); the Russian Imperial Ballet, choreography: Ivanov, Cecchetti, St. Petersburg, Dec. 5, 1893 (a still earlier Russian *Cinderella* was staged in Moscow, Jan. 6, 1825); Original Ballet Russe, choreography: Michel Fokine; music: Frederic d'Erlanger; scenery and costumes: Nathalie Gontcharova, first presented in London, July 19, 1938, and in New York, Nov. 16, 1940. (As *Cendrillon*, produced May 8, 1815, St. Petersburg; produced May 13, 1823, Paris Opera, with choreography by Didelot; in these and subsequent productions, various choreographers, composers, designers were employed; Russian title for *Cinderella* is *Zolushka*.)

Le Combat (See *The Duel*)

Con Amore

Choreography: Lew Christensen; music: Rossini; libretto: James Graham-Lujan; scenery and costumes: James Bodrero. First produced by the San Francisco Ballet in its home city, Mar. 10, 1953. Added to the repertory of the New York City Ballet, New York, June 9, 1953. The scenery and costumes for the New York City Ballet production were designed by Esteban Frances.

The Concert

Choreography: Jerome Robbins; music: Chopin (various selections); costumes: Irene Sharaff. First produced by the New York City Ballet, New York, Mar. 6, 1956. Extensively revised and restaged (with décor by Saul Steinberg) by Robbins for his Ballets: U.S.A., Spoleto, Italy, June 8, 1958; New York, Sept. 4, 1958.

Concerto

Choreography: Kenneth MacMillan; music: Shostakovich (Concerto Piano No. 2, Op. 102); costumes: Jürgen Rose. First produced by the Deutsche Oper Ballet, West Berlin, Nov. 11, 1966. First American production by the American Ballet Theatre, New York, May 18, 1967. Added to the repertory of the Royal Ballet, London, May 26, 1967.

Concerto Barocco

Choreography: George Balanchine; music: Bach (Concerto in D Minor for Two Violins); scenery and costumes: Eugene Berman. First produced by the American Ballet, New York, May 29, 1941. Presented by the Ballet Russe de Monte Carlo, New York, Sept. 9, 1945, without the Berman scenery and costumes. Added to the repertory of the Marquis de Cuevas' Grand Ballet, 1948, in Europe. Revived by the New York City Ballet, New York, Oct. 11, 1948, with original Berman setting and costumes. Restaged by the New York City Ballet, New York, Sept. 13, 1951, without the Berman scenery and costumes and using instead (as did the Ballet Russe) black practice costumes and an unadorned cyclorama as a background. The ballet is also in the repertory of the San Francisco Ballet.

Constantia
Choreography: William Dollar; music: Chopin (Piano Concerto in F Minor); scenery: Horace Armistead; costumes: Grace Houston. First produced by the Ballet International, New York, Oct. 31, 1944. Added to the repertory of the Original Ballet Russe, New York, Oct. 16, 1946. Staged by the Marquis de Cuevas' Grand Ballet, 1947-1948. Remounted by Ballet Theatre (now the American Ballet Theatre), New York, Apr. 9, 1951, with scenery and costumes by Robert Davison.

Coppélia
Choreography: Arthur Saint-Léon; music: Léo Delibes; book: Charles Nuitter and Saint-Léon. First presented at the Paris Opera, May 25, 1870. First American performance by the National (formerly, American) Opera Company, New York, Mar. 11, 1887 (possibly seen earlier on tour), in a production staged by Mamert Bibeyran. First presented in St. Petersburg in 1884 by the Russian Imperial Ballet with Saint-Léon choreography as reconstructed by Marius Petipa. Produced by the Royal Danish Ballet, Copenhagen, Dec. 27, 1896, in a version adapted from the Saint-Léon original by Hans Beck (later revised by Harald Lander). The Russian version of *Coppélia* was first performed in America by Anna Pavlova and Mikhail Mordkin, with the Metropolitan Opera Ballet, in New York (at the Met.), Feb. 28, 1910. The ballet was first danced in London in 1906 in a production starring Adeline Genée. While the contemporary French and Danish stagings of *Coppélia* are direct descendants of the Saint-Léon original, the English and American mountings derive from the Imperial Russian version. The Vic-Wells Ballet presented it in London, Mar. 21, 1933; as the Sadler's Wells Ballet, restaged it Oct. 25, 1946; and the junior company, the Sadler's Wells Theatre Ballet, presented a new production in London, Sept. 4, 1951, and performed it in New York, Mar. 27, 1952. The Ballet Russe de Monte Carlo production, staged by Sergueff after Petipa, Ivanov, and Cecchetti, was presented in London in Sept., 1938, and given its first New York performance Oct. 17, 1938. A shortened *Coppélia*, arranged by Simon Semenoff, was

produced by Ballet Theatre (now the American Ballet Theatre), New York, Oct. 22, 1942. A production of *Coppélia*, staged by Ivan Clustine, was in the repertory of Anna Pavlova and her touring company. There have been and are many other mountings of this perennial ballet favorite.

Le Coq d'Or

Choreography: Michel Fokine; music: Rimsky-Korsakoff; based on the Rimsky-Korsakoff opera, with libretto by Byelsky, suggested by a poem of Pushkin; scenery and costumes: Nathalie Gontcharova. First produced by the Ballet Russe de Monte Carlo, New York, Oct. 23, 1937. Earlier productions included one as an opera-pantomime presented by Diaghileff in Paris, May 21, 1914. On Mar. 6, 1918, an opera pantomime staging by Adolph Bolm was given at the Metropolitan Opera House.

Danse Concertantes

Choreography: George Balanchine; music: Igor Stravinsky; scenery and costumes: Eugene Berman. First produced by the Ballet Russe de Monte Carlo, New York, Sept. 10, 1944. Another version of the Ballet, with totally different choreography by Kenneth MacMillan and scenery and costumes of Nicholas Georgiadis, was presented by the Sadler's Wells Theatre Ballet, London, Jan. 18, 1955.

Daphnis and Chloë

Choreography and book: Michel Fokine; music: Maurice Ravel; scenery and costumes: Léon Bakst. First produced by Diaghileff's Ballets Russes, Paris, June 8, 1912. In 1936 the Philadelphia Ballet produced *Daphnis and Chloë*, with new choreography by Catherine Littlefield. On Apr. 5, 1951, in London, the Sadler's Wells Ballet (now the Royal Ballet) presented *Daphnis and Chloë*, with wholly new choreography by Frederick Ashton and scenery and costumes by John Craxton. The Ashton ballet had its American première by the same company, New York, Sept. 25, 1953.

Dark Elegies

Choreography: Antony Tudor; music: Gustav Mahler (Kindertotenlieder); scenery and costumes: Nadia Benois. First produced by the Ballet Rambert, London, Feb. 19, 1937, and later presented by the Vic-Wells Ballet. First American production by Ballet Theatre (now the American Ballet Theatre), New York, Jan. 24, 1940, with scenery and costumes by Raymond Sovey based on the Benois originals. Also in the repertory of the National Ballet of Canada.

Death and the Maiden

Choreography: André Howard; music: Franz Schubert; costumes: Andrée Howard. First produced by the Ballet Rambert, London,

Feb. 23, 1937. Restaged by Ballet Theatre (now the American Ballet Theatre), New York, Jan. 18, 1940.

Les Demoiselles de la Nuit (The Ladies of Midnight)
Choreography: Roland Petit; music: Jean Françaix; book: Jean Anouilh; scenery and costumes: Léonor Fini. First produced by Roland Petit's Ballets de Paris, Paris, May 21, 1948. First presented in America by Ballet Theatre (now the American Ballet Theatre), Apr. 13, 1951.

Designs with Strings
Choreography: John Taras; music: Tchaikovsky (second movement of Trio in A Minor); costumes (for the American presentation): Irene Sharaff. First produced by the Metropolitan Ballet, Edinburgh, Scotland, Feb. 6, 1948. American première by Ballet Theatre (now the American Ballet Theatre), New York, Apr. 25, 1950.

Devil's Holiday
Choreography: Frederick Ashton; book and music (on themes of Paganini): Vincenzo Tommasini; scenery and costumes: Eugene Berman. First produced by the Ballet Russe de Monte Carlo, New York, Oct. 26, 1939.

Dim Lustre
Choreography: Antony Tudor; music: Richard Strauss (Burlesca); scenery and costumes: Motley. First produced by Ballet Theatre (now the American Ballet Theatre), New York, Oct. 20, 1943. Produced by the New York City Ballet, with scenery and costumes by Beni Montresor. First performance, New York, May 6, 1964.

Divertimento
Choreography: George Balanchine; music: Alexi Haieff; practice costumes. First produced by the Ballet Society, New York, Jan. 13, 1947, continuing in the repertory of the New York City Ballet.

Divertimento No. 15 (formerly called *Caracole*)
Choreography: George Balanchine; music: Mozart; costumes: Christian Bérard. First produced by the New York City Ballet under the title *Caracole*, New York, Feb. 19, 1952. Using the musical title *Divertimento No. 15*, the ballet, with entirely new choreography by Balanchine, was presented as a new work by the New York City Ballet in New York, Dec. 19, 1956. The reason for the new version had nothing to do with the merits of *Caracole*, which had been a success; while *Caracole* was resting from repertory duty for a few seasons, the choreographer forgot his original choreography (and the dancers did also) and was compelled to create a wholly new ballet to the same music. The production was also new, with costumes by Karinska and a setting borrowed from Symphonie Concertante, by James Stewart Morcom.

Don Juan

Choreography: Michel Fokine; music: Gluck; scenery and costumes: Mariano Andreù; based on Gluck's ballet (derived from the Molière play), first presented in Vienna, 1761, with choreography by Angiolini. The Fokine ballet was given by the Ballet Russe de Monte Carlo, London, June 25, 1936, and in New York, Oct. 22, 1938.

Don Quixote (or Don Quichotte)

Choreography: Marius Petipa; music: Leon Minkus; libretto: Petipa, based on the Cervantes novel. First produced by the Russian Imperial Ballet, Dec. 14, 1869, in four acts and eight scenes. A later staging of the Petipa ballet in five acts and eleven scenes was presented in St. Petersburg, Nov. 9 (Julian or Russian calendar) or Nov. 21 (Gregorian or Western calendar), 1871, and a revised version by Gorsky was given in Moscow, Jan. 20 (Julian) or Feb. 2 (Gregorian), 1902. *Don Quixote* remains in the repertories of the Soviet State Ballet. *Don Quichotte Chez la Duchesse,* a three-act comic ballet, was produced in Paris, Feb. 12, 1743. A version of the Petipa-Minkus ballet, staged by Laurent Novikoff in a prologue and two acts, was in the repertory of Anna Pavlova's company. A contemporary *Don Quixote,* with choreography by Ninette de Valois, music by Robert Gerhard and scenery and costumes by Edward Burra, was produced by the Sadler's Wells Ballet (now the Royal Ballet), London, Feb. 20, 1950, and Sept. 29, 1950, in New York. In America an entirely new production, with choreography by George Balanchine, music by Nicholas Nabokov, scenery, costumes (executed by Karinska), and lighting by Esteban Frances (assisted by Peter Harvey), was given its world première in New York, May 28, 1965. The ballet, in a prologue and three acts, was the first full-length ballet choreographed by Balanchine to a commissioned score. The choreographer danced the title role himself at a benefit preview, May 27, 1965. Other historical productions of *Don Quixote* include one by Jean Georges Noverre in the mid-eighteenth century and one by Paul Taglioni in the 1830's.

Donizetti Variations (Variations from Don Sebastian)

Choreography: George Balanchine; music: Gaetano Donizetti; costumes: Karinska and Esteban Frances. First presented by the New York City Ballet, New York, Nov. 16, 1960. Added to the repertory of the Robert Joffrey Ballet (now the City Center Joffrey Ballet), with costumes by William Pitkin, New York, Sept. 15, 1966.

The Dream

Choreography: Frederick Ashton; music: Felix Mendelssohn; scenery: Henry Bardon; costumes: David Walker. First presented by the Royal Ballet, London, Apr. 2, 1964; presented by the same company in America, New York, Apr. 30, 1965. The ballet is based on Shakespeare's play *A Midsummer Night's Dream*.

Dream Pictures
Choreography: Emilie Walbom; music: Hans Christian Lumbye; scenery and costumes reproduce Copenhagen's Tivoli Gardens in the Biedermeier period. First produced by the Royal Danish Ballet, Copenhagen, Apr. 15, 1915. First full-scale American presentation by the same company, New York, Sept. 19, 1956. In the summer of 1955, an abridged version was given at the Jacob's Pillow Dance Festival at Lee, Mass., and at New York's Lewisohn Stadium.

The Duel (also *Le Combat* and *The Combat*)
Choreography: William Dollar; music: Rafaello de Banfield. First seen in America as *Le Combat* by Roland Petit's Ballets de Paris, New York, Oct. 6, 1949. First presented in a revised and enlarged version as *The Duel* by the New York City Ballet, New York, Feb. 24, 1950. As *The Combat*, with scenery and costumes by Georges Wakhevitch, it was added to the repertory of Ballet Theatre (now the American Ballet Theatre), London, July 23, 1953. The Petit production, which had its world première in London, Feb. 24, 1949, was an elaborate *pas de deux*. The New York City Ballet production, with costumes by Robert Stevenson, was rechoreographed to include three supporting male dancers in addition to the two principals.

The Dying Swan (or *Le Cygne*)
Choreography: Michel Fokine; music: Camille Saint-Saëns. First produced in 1905 in St. Petersburg at a concert and danced by Anna Pavlova.

Echoing of Trumpets (Echoes of Trumpets)
Choreography: Antony Tudor; music: Bohuslav Martinu (Fantasie Symphonique); scenery: Birger Bergling. First presented by the Royal Swedish Ballet, Stockholm, Sept. 28, 1963. First presented in America by the Metropolitan Opera Ballet, New York, Mar. 27, 1966.

Les Elfes (The Elves)
Choreography: Michel Fokine; music: Felix Mendelssohn (Overture to *A Midsummer Night's Dream*, Andante and Allegro from Concerto in E Minor for Violin). First produced by the Fokine Ballet, New York, Feb. 26, 1924. Restaged, with costumes by Christian Bérard, by the Ballet Russe de Monte Carlo at Monte Carlo, Apr. 24, 1937. Revived by the same company in America, Mar. 22, 1939. Later revived by the same company, New York, Apr. 20, 1950.

Episodes
Choreography: Martha Graham and George Balanchine; music:

Anton Webern (Passacaglia, Opus 1; Six Pieces, Opus 6; Symphony, Opus 21; Five Pieces, Opus 10; Concerto, Opus 24; Variations, Opus 30; Ricercata in Six Voices from Bach's Musical Offering); costumes, Karinska; scenery: David Hays. First produced by the New York City Ballet, New York, May 14, 1959. The Balanchine section alone, under the same title, remains in the repertory of the New York City Ballet.

La Esmeralda

Choreography and book: Jules Perrot; music: Cesare Pugni; scenery: W. Grieve; costumes: Mme. Copère. First produced in London, Mar. 9, 1844. First presented in America by the Monplaisir Ballet Company, New York, Sept. 18, 1848. Russian première, St. Petersburg, Dec. 21 (Julian or Russian calendar), 1848, or Jan. 2 (Gregorian or Western calendar), 1849. Restaged in 1954 by the London Festival Ballet, London, with choreography by Nicholas Beriosoff and presented in America as a divertissement (Act II) on a tour, with the New York (Brooklyn) première taking place Feb. 18, 1955. *Esmeralda* remains in the repertory of the Soviet State Ballet.

Études

Choreography: Harald Lander; music: Karl Czerny (Études, arr. by Knudage Riisager). First presented by the Royal Danish Ballet, Copenhagen, Jan. 15, 1948. First produced by the American Ballet Theatre, with scenery and costumes by Rolf Gerard (executed by Karinska), New York, Oct. 5, 1961. Other productions include those of Festival Ballet, London, July 11, 1956, and the Paris Opera, Paris, Nov. 19, 1952.

Façade

Choreography: Frederick Ashton; music: William Walton; scenery and costumes: John Armstrong; based upon poems by Edith Sitwell. First performed by the Camargo Society, London, Apr. 26, 1931. Presented by the Ballet Rambert, London, May 4, 1931. Added to the repertory of the Sadler's Wells Ballet (now the Royal Ballet), London, Oct. 8, 1935. First presented by the Sadler's Wells Ballet in America, New York, Oct. 12, 1949.

Fall River Legend

Choreography: Agnes de Mille; music: Morton Gould; scenery: Oliver Smith; costumes: Miles White. First produced by Ballet Theatre (now the American Ballet Theatre), New York, Apr. 22, 1948.

Fancy Free

Choreography: Jerome Robbins; music: Leonard Bernstein; scenery and costumes: Oliver Smith. First produced by Ballet Theatre (now the American Ballet Theatre), New York, Apr. 18, 1944.

Fanfare

Choreography: Jerome Robbins; music: Benjamin Britten (The Young Person's Guide to the Orchestra); scenery and costumes: Irene Sharaff. First produced by the New York City Ballet, New York, June 2, 1953. Added to the repertory of the Royal Danish Ballet, Copenhagen, Apr. 29, 1956.

The Fantastic Toyshop (See *La Boutique Fantasque*)

La Fille Mal Gardée (*The Unchaperoned Daughter*) Also presented in Russia as *Useless Precautions* and in America, in the past, as *The Wayward Daughter* and *Naughty Lisette*.

Choreography and libretto: Jean Dauberval; music: Peter Ludwig Hertel. First produced in Bordeaux, France, in 1786 (often called the oldest ballet extant). First performed in America early in the 19th century. Revived in New York by the Mordkin Ballet, 1937 (first New York performance, Nov. 12, 1938), and restaged Jan. 19, 1940, in New York by Ballet Theatre (now the American Ballet Theatre), with choreographic revisions by Bronislava Nijinska and scenery and costumes by Serge Soudeikine. An entirely new production with choreography by Frederick Ashton, music by Ferdinand Hérold (adt. by John Lanchbery), and scenery and costumes by Osbert Lancaster was presented by the Royal Ballet, London, Jan. 28, 1960. First presented in America by the same company in New York, Sept. 14, 1960. This version entered the repertory of the Royal Danish Ballet, Copenhagen, Jan. 16, 1964.

Fille Mal Gardée (*Nault after Dauberval*)

Choreography: Ferdinand Nault, after Dauberval; music: P. L. Hertel; décor and costumes: William Pitkin. First performance, Nault version: April 2, 1966, Robert Joffrey Ballet, New York City Center.

Filling Station

Choreography: Lew Christensen; music: Virgil Thomson; book: Lincoln Kirstein; scenery and costumes: Paul Cadmus. First produced by the Ballet Caravan, Hartford, Conn., Jan. 6, 1938. Revived by the New York City Ballet, New York, May 12, 1953.

Le Fils Prodigue (See *The Prodigal Son*)

Firebird (*L'Oiseau de Feu*)

Choreography: Michel Fokine; music: Igor Stravinsky; scenery and costumes: Golovine. First produced by Diaghileff's Ballets Russes, Paris, June 25, 1910. First presented in America by the same company, Jan. 17, 1916. Revived in 1926, with scenery and costumes by Nathalie Gontcharova. Presented by the Ballet Russe de Monte Carlo, New York, Mar. 20, 1935, and presented by the Original Ballet Russe, New York, Dec. 6, 1940, both productions using the

Gontcharova settings and costumes. Restaged, with choreography by Adolph Bolm and scenery and costumes by Marc Chagall, by Ballet Theatre (now the American Ballet Theatre), New York, Oct. 24, 1945. Produced by the New York City Ballet, with new choreography by George Balanchine and with the Chagall settings and costumes, Nov. 27, 1949. The Fokine original, staged by Serge Grigoriev and Lubov Tchernicheva (members of the Diaghileff company), with scenery and costumes by Gontcharova, was produced by the Sadler's Wells Ballet (now the Royal Ballet), Edinburgh, Aug. 23, 1954, and presented in New York, Sept. 20, 1955.

The Flames of Paris

Choreography: V. Vynonen; music: B. V. Assafiev; scenery: V. V. Dmitriev; mime: S. Radlov. First produced, Leningrad, Nov. 7, 1932.

The Fountain of Bakhchisarai

Choreography: R. Zakharoff; music: B. Asafiev; book (based on a poem of Pushkin): N. Volkoff; scenery: V. M. Khodasevich. First produced in Leningrad, 1934.

The Four Temperaments

Choreography: George Balanchine; music: Paul Hindemith; scenery and costumes: Kurt Seligmann. First produced by Ballet Society (later the New York City Ballet), New York, Nov. 20, 1946. Revived by the New York City Ballet, Oct. 25, 1948, and, in Nov. of 1952, the scenery and costumes were discarded in favor of a plain backdrop and simple practice clothes.

A la Françaix

Choreography: George Balanchine; music: Jean Françaix. First produced by the New York City Ballet, New York, Sept. 11, 1951.

Frankie and Johnny

Choreography: Ruth Page and Bentley Stone; music: Jerome Moross; book: Michael Blandford and Moross; scenery and costumes: Paul Dupont. First produced by the Page-Stone Ballet for the dance theater project of the Works Progress Administration, Chicago, June 19, 1938. Restaged, with new scenery by Clive Rickabaugh, for the Ballet Russe de Monte Carlo, New York, Feb. 28, 1945.

Gaité Parisienne

Choreography: Leonide Massine; music: Jacques Offenbach; book, scenery and costumes: Comte Etienne de Beaumont. First produced by the Ballet Russe de Monte Carlo, at Monte Carlo, Apr. 5, 1938. First American performance by the same company, New York, Oct. 12, 1938.

Gala Performance
Choreography: Antony Tudor; music: Serge Prokofieff; scenery and costumes: Hugh Stevenson. First produced by the London Ballet, London, Dec. 5, 1938. First presented in America by Ballet Theatre (now the American Ballet Theatre), with scenery and costumes by Nicolas de Molas, New York, Feb. 11, 1941.

Giselle
Choreography: Jean Coralli and Jules Perrot; music: Adolphe Adam; book: Coralli, Théophile Gautier, and Vernoy de Saint-George; scenery: Pierre Ciceri; costumes: Paul Lormier. First presented in Paris, June 28, 1841. London première, Mar. 12, 1842; St. Petersburg première, Dec. 18, 1842; American première, Boston, Jan. 1, 1846.

Gounod Symphony
Choreography: George Balanchine; music: Charles Gounod (Symphony No. 1); scenery: Horace Armistead; costumes: Karinska. First produced by the New York City Ballet, New York, Jan. 8, 1958.

Graduation Ball
Choreography: David Lichine; music: Johann Strauss; scenery and costumes: Alexandre Benois. First produced by the Original Ballet Russe, Sydney, Australia, Feb. 28, 1940. First American performance, Los Angeles, Nov. 10, 1940. Presented by Ballet Theatre (now the American Ballet Theatre), with scenery and costumes by Mstislav Doboujinsky, New York, Oct. 8, 1944. Also in the repertory of the Royal Danish Ballet.

Grand Pas–Glazounov (See *Pas de Dix*)

Harbinger
Choreography: Eliot Feld; music: Serge Prokofieff (Piano Concerto No. 5 in G Major, Op. 55, excluding the first movement); scenery: Oliver Smith; costumes: Stanley Simmons. First New York performance by the American Ballet Theatre, May 11, 1967 (the ballet had been previewed during the company's spring United States tour).

Harlequinade
Choreography: George Balanchine; music: Riccardo Drigo (Harlequin's Millions); scenery and costumes: Rouben Ter-Artunian. First presented by the New York City Ballet, New York, Feb. 4, 1965.

Helen of Troy
Choreography and book: David Lichine; music: Jacques Offenbach; scenery and costumes: Marcel Vertès. First produced by Ballet Theatre (now the American Ballet Theatre), Mexico City,

Sept. 10, 1942; first United States performance, Detroit, Nov. 29, 1942.

Homage to the Queen
Choreography: Frederick Ashton; music: Malcolm Arnold; scenery and costumes: Oliver Messel. First produced by the Sadler's Wells Ballet (now the Royal Ballet), London, June 2, 1953. First presented in America by the same company, New York, Sept. 18, 1953.

Illuminations
Choreography: Frederick Ashton; music: Benjamin Britten; poems (set by Britten): Arthur Rimbaud; scenery and costumes: Cecil Beaton. First produced by the New York City Ballet, New York, Mar. 2, 1950.

Interplay
Choreography: Jerome Robbins; music: Morton Gould. First presented in Billy Rose's production, *Concert Varieties*, New York, June 1, 1945. Added to the repertory of Ballet Theatre (now the American Ballet Theatre), New York, Oct. 17, 1945, with setting by Oliver Smith and costumes by Irene Sharaff. Added to the repertory of the New York City Ballet, New York, Dec. 23, 1952.

The Invitation
Choreography: Kenneth MacMillan; music: Matyas Seiber; scenery and costumes: Nicholas Georgiadis. First presented by the Royal Ballet, Oxford, Nov. 10, 1960; first London performance, Dec. 30, 1960. First performance in America by the same company, New York, May 10, 1963.

Ivesiana
Choreography: George Balanchine; music: Charles Ives. First produced by the New York City Ballet, New York, Sept. 14, 1954.

Jardin aux Lilas (Lilac Garden)
Choreography: Antony Tudor; music: Ernest Chausson (Poème); scenery and costumes: Hugh Stevenson. First produced by the Ballet Rambert, London, Jan. 26, 1936. First presented in America by Ballet Theatre (now the American Ballet Theatre), New York, Jan. 15, 1940. Added to the repertory of the New York City Ballet, with setting by Horace Armistead and costumes by Karinska, New York, Nov. 30, 1951.

Le Jeune Homme et la Mort (The Young Man and Death)
Choreography: Roland Petit; music: Bach (Passacaglia and Fugue in C Minor); book: Jean Cocteau; scenery and costumes: Georges Wakhevitch. First produced by the Ballets des Champs-Elysées, Paris, June 25, 1946. First presented in America by Ballet Theatre (now the American Ballet Theatre), New York, Apr. 9, 1951.

Jeux (Games)
Choreography: Vaslav Nijinsky; music: Claude Debussy; scenery
and costumes: Léon Bakst. First presented by the Diaghileff Ballets
Russes, Paris, May 15, 1913. Presented in America with new cho-
reography by Wiliam Dollar and scenery and costumes by David
Ffolkes by Ballet Theatre (now the American Ballet Theatre), New
York, Apr. 23, 1950. A new version with choreography by John
Taras, using the Nijinsky libretto, and with décor by Raoul Pène
du Bois was presented by the New York City Ballet, New York,
Apr. 28, 1966.

The Jewels
Choreography: George Balanchine; music: Gabriel Fauré ("Pelléas
et Mélisande" and "Shylock"); Igor Stravinsky (Capriccio for Piano
and Orchestra) and Tchaikovsky (Symphony No. 3 in D Major);
scenery: Peter Harvey; costumes: Karinska. First presented by the
New York City Ballet, New York, Apr. 13, 1967. Each of the ballet's three sections is named after a precious stone: Emeralds
(Fauré), Rubies (Stravinsky), and Diamonds (Tchaikovsky).

Jinx
Choreography: Lew Christensen; music: Benjamin Britten (Var-
iations on a Theme by Frank Bridge); scenery: James Stewart
Morcum; costumes: Felipe Fiocca. First produced by the Dance
Players, New York, Apr. 24, 1942. Restaged by the New York City
Ballet, New York, Nov. 24, 1949. Also in the repertory of the San
Francisco Ballet.

Judgment of Paris
Choreography: Antony Tudor; music: Kurt Weill; costumes: Hugh
Laing. First produced by the Ballet Rambert, London, June 15,
1938. First presented in America, with scenery and costumes by
Lucinda Ballard, by Ballet Theatre (now the American Ballet
Theatre), New York, Jan. 20, 1940.

Konservatoriet
Choreography: August Bournonville; music: Paulli. First produced
as a two-act work by the Royal Danish Ballet, 1849. Revived in
one-act form (without plot) at a later date and first presented in
America by the Royal Danish Ballet, New York, Sept. 29, 1956.

Le Lac des Cygnes (See *Swan Lake*)

The Lesson (also *The Private Lesson*)
Choreography: Flemming Flindt; music: Georges Delerue; libretto:
Eugene Ionesco, based on his play, *The Private Lesson*; scenery:
Bernard Daydé. First presented at the Opéra Comique, Paris, Apr.
6, 1964. First American performance by the Royal Danish Ballet,
New York, Dec. 7, 1965. First produced as a television ballet,

The Lesson is also in the repertory of Ruth Page's Chicago Opera Ballet.

Liebeslieder Walzer
Choreography: George Balanchine; music: Johannes Brahms (Liebeslieder Walzer, Op. 52 and Op. 65, for vocal quartet and duo pianists); scenery: David Hays; costumes: Karinska. First presented by the New York City Ballet, New York, Nov. 22, 1960.

Meditation
Choreography: George Balanchine; music: Tchaikovsky; costumes: Karinska. First presented by the New York City Ballet, New York, Dec. 10, 1963.

A Midsummer Night's Dream
Choreography: George Balanchine; music: Felix Mendelssohn (Overture and Incidental music to "A Midsummer Night's Dream"; Overtures to "Son and Stranger," "Athalie," "Fair Melusine"; Symphony for Strings, No. 9; "The First Walpurgis Night"); scenery and lighting: David Hays (assisted by Peter Harvey); costumes: Karinska. First presented by the New York City Ballet, New York, Jan. 17, 1962. In two acts, this was Balanchine's second full-length ballet, the first after *The Nutcracker* (1954). The action is based upon Shakespeare's play of the same title.

Miss Julie
Choreography: Birgit Cullberg; music: Ture Rangstrom; scenery and costumes: Sven Erixon. First produced by the Royal Swedish Opera Ballet, Vasteras, Sweden, Mar. 1, 1950. First presented in America by the American Ballet Theatre, New York, Sept. 18, 1958.

Monumentum pro Gesualdo
Choreography: George Balanchine; music: Igor Stravinsky (Three Madrigals by Gesualdo di Venoso recomposed for Instruments); scenery: David Hays. First presented by the New York City Ballet, New York, Nov. 16, 1960.

Moonreindeer
Choreography: Birgit Cullberg; music: Knudager Riisager; décor and costumes: Per Falk. First produced by the Royal Danish Ballet, Copenhagen, Nov. 22, 1957. This production first presented in America by the American Ballet Theatre, New York, Oct. 10, 1961. The ballet is also in the repertory of the Royal Swedish Ballet.

Movements for Piano and Orchestra
Choreography: George Balanchine; music: Igor Stravinsky (Movements for Piano and Orchestra). First presented by the New York City Ballet, New York, Apr. 9, 1963.

Moves
Choreography: Jerome Robbins. First performed by his Ballets:

U.S.A., Spoleto, Italy, July 3, 1959. First presented by the same company in America, New York, Oct. 8, 1961. In this work, Robbins used no music; the entire ballet is danced in silence.

Napoli (or *The Fisherman and His Bride*)
Choreography and book: August Bournonville; music: Paulli, Helsted, Gade; scenery: Christensen. First produced by the Royal Danish Ballet, Copenhagen, Mar. 29, 1842. First presented in America by the Royal Danish Ballet, New York, Sept. 18, 1956. A one-act divertissement version of the ballet, arranged by Harald Lander, was mounted for the London Festival Ballet, London, 1954, and presented in America during a 1954-1955 tour.

Narkissos
Choreography: Edward Villella; music: Robert Prince; book: William D. Roberts; décor and costumes: John Braden. First performance: July 21, 1966, Saratoga Springs, New York, N.Y., Performing Arts Center, New York City Ballet; first New York performance: Nov. 24, 1966, New York City Ballet, New York State Theater.

N.Y. Export, Op. Jazz
Choreography: Jerome Robbins; music: Robert Prince; décor: Ben Shahn; costumes: Florence Klotz. First produced for the Festival of Two Worlds, Spoleto, Italy, June 8, 1958, by Mr. Robbins' own company, Ballets: U.S.A. First presented in New York City by the same company, Sept. 4, 1958.

Night Shadow (also *La Sonnambula*)
Choreography: George Balanchine; music: Vittorio Rieti (on themes of Bellini); scenery and costumes: Dorothea Tanning. First produced by the Ballet Russe de Monte Carlo, New York, Feb. 27, 1946. Added to the repertory of the Marquis de Cuevas' Grand Ballet, London, Aug. 26, 1948. As *La Sonnambula*, the ballet with the Balanchine choreography was produced by John Taras, with scenery and costumes by André Delfau, for the Royal Danish Ballet, Copenhagen, Jan. 9, 1955, and presented in New York, Sept. 21, 1956. Produced by the New York City Ballet (staged by Taras), New York, Jan. 6, 1960.

Les Noces (The Wedding)
Choreography: Bronislava Nijinska; music and words: Igor Stravinsky; scenery and costumes: Nathalie Gontcharova. First produced by Diaghileff's Ballets Russes, Paris, June 13, 1923. First presented in America, with choreography by Elizaveta Anderson-Ivantzova, by the League of American Composers, New York, Apr. 25, 1929. The Nijinska original was revised by the Ballet Russe de Monte Carlo in April, 1936, and presented during that company's American tour; also revived by the choreographer for the Royal Ballet,

London, Mar. 23, 1966, and presented by the same company during their American tour, New York, May 2, 1967. An entirely new production with choreography by Jerome Robbins, scenery by Oliver Smith, and costumes by Patricia Zipprodt received its first performance in New York, Mar. 30, 1965, presented by the American Ballet Theatre.

The Nutcracker (Casse Noisette)
Choreography: Lev Ivanov, following the projected plan of Marius Petipa; music: Tchaikovsky; scenery: Botcharov. First produced by the Russian Imperial Ballet, St. Petersburg, Dec. 5 (Julian or Russian calendar) or Dec. 17 (Gregorian or Western calendar), 1892. First presented in Western Europe, with choreography by Nicholas Sergeyev after the Ivanov original and with costumes by Hedley Briggs, by the Sadler's Wells Ballet (now the Royal Ballet), London, Jan. 30, 1934. First presented in America, with scenery and costumes by Alexandre Benois, by the Ballet Russe de Monte Carlo, New York, Oct. 17, 1940. Restaged, with choreography by George Balanchine, settings by Horace Armistead and costumes by Karinska, by the New York City Ballet, New York, Feb. 2, 1954; revised version, with new scenery by Rouben Ter-Artunian, was first presented in New York, Dec. 11, 1964. Also performed by other companies in different versions. The *pas de deux* for the Sugar Plum Fairy and the Prince is frequently given separately from the ballet itself as a divertissement for the ballerina and a cavalier. *The Nutcracker* is a Christmas ballet based upon the story by E. T. A. Hoffmann, "The Nutcracker and the King of the Mice."

L'Oiseau de Feu (See *The Firebird*)

Olympics
Choreography: Gerald Arpino; music: Toshiro Mayuzumi. First presented by the Robert Joffrey Ballet (now the City Center Joffrey Ballet), New York, Mar. 31, 1965.

Ondine
Choreography: Frederick Ashton; music: Hans Werner Henze; scenery and costumes: Lila de Nobili. First presented by the Royal Ballet, London, Oct. 27, 1958; presented by the same company for the first time in America in New York, Sept. 21, 1960.

Orpheus
Choreography: George Balanchine; music: Igor Stravinsky; scenery and costumes: Isamu Noguchi. First produced by the Ballet Society (now the New York City Ballet), New York, Apr. 28, 1948.

Paradise Lost
Choreography: Roland Petit; music: Marius Constant; scenery and costumes: Martial Raysse; based on an 'argument' by Jean Cau.

First presented by the Royal Ballet, London, Feb. 23, 1967; performed by the same company for the first time in America, May 10, 1967.

Pas de Dix
Choreography: George Balanchine; music: Alexander Glazounov; costumes: Esteban Frances. First produced by the New York City Ballet, New York, Nov. 9, 1955. Restaged for the American Ballet Theatre by Frederic Franklin under the title *Grand Pas—Glazounov,* New York, Apr. 25, 1961.

Pas de Quatre
Choreography: Jules Perrot; music: Cesare Pugni. First produced in London, July 12, 1845, the first of four performances, one a command performance for Queen Victoria. Revived, with a single change of cast (Carolina Rosati replacing Lucile Grahn), in 1847. Keith Lester re-created *Pas de Quatre* in London in 1936 for the Markova-Dolin Ballet, Anton Dolin arranged a new version of the work for Ballet Theatre (now the American Ballet Theatre), New York, Feb. 16, 1941. Later, the Ballet Russe de Monte Carlo presented the Dolin version and Ballet Theatre presented the Lester staging.

Pas de Trois (Glinka)
Choreography: George Balanchine; music: Michael Glinka; costumes: Karinska. First produced by the New York City Ballet, New York, Mar. 1, 1955.

Pas de Trois (Minkus)
Choreography: George Balanchine; music: Léon Minkus; costumes: Karinska. First produced by the New York City Ballet, Feb. 18, 1951. An earlier presentation of this short work, set to music from the Minkus score for the full-length *Don Quixote,* was presented by the Marquis de Cuevas' Grand Ballet.

Pas des Déesses
Choreography: Robert Joffrey; music: John Field. First produced by the Robert Joffrey Ballet (now the City Center Joffrey Ballet), New York, May 29, 1954. Staged by Joffrey for the Ballet Rambert, London, June 30, 1955. Presented by Ballet Theatre (now the American Ballet Theatre), New York, May 7, 1956.

Pastorale
Choreography: Francisco Moncion; music: Charles Turner (his first score for ballet); scenery: David Hays; costumes: Ruth Sobotka. First produced by the New York City Ballet, New York, Feb. 14, 1957.

Les Patineurs (The Skaters)
Choreography: Frederick Ashton; music: Giacomo Meyerbeer, ar-

ranged by Constant Lambert from themes from Meyerbeer's operas; scenery and costumes: William Chappell. First produced by the Sadler's Wells Ballet (now the Royal Ballet), London, Feb. 16, 1937. First produced in America, with scenery and costumes by Cecil Beaton, by Ballet Theatre (now the American Ballet Theatre), New York, Oct. 2, 1946.

La Péri

Choreography: Frederick Ashton; music: Paul Dukas; scenery and costumes: André Levasseur. First produced by the Sadler's Wells Ballet (now the Royal Ballet), London, Feb. 15, 1956. First presented in America by the same company, New York, Sept. 26, 1957.

Peter and the Wolf

Choreography: Adolph Bolm; music and book: Serge Prokofieff; scenery and costumes: Lucinda Ballard. First produced by Ballet Theatre (now the American Ballet Theatre), New York, Jan. 13, 1940.

Petrouchka

Choreography: Michel Fokine; music: Igor Stravinsky; book: Stravinsky and Alexandre Benois; scenery and costumes: Benois. First produced by Diaghileff's Ballets Russes, Paris, June 13, 1911. First presented in America by the same company, New York, Jan. 24, 1916. First mounted (under Fokine's direction) by the Royal Danish Ballet, Copenhagen, Oct. 14, 1925. The Ballet Russe de Monte Carlo's production was first presented in New York, Jan. 10, 1934. Staged by Ballet Theatre (now the American Ballet Theatre), under Fokine's direction, New York, Oct. 8, 1942. Also in the repertory of the Original Ballet Russe, Britain's Royal Ballet and other companies.

The Pied Piper

Choreography: Jerome Robbins; music: Aaron Copland (Concerto for Clarinet and String Orchestra). First produced by the New York City Ballet, New York, Dec. 4, 1951.

Piège de Lumière

Choreography: John Taras; music: Jean-Michel Damase; libretto: Philippe Hériate; scenery: Felix Labisse; costumes: André Levasseur. First performed by the Marquis de Cuevas' Grand Ballet, Paris, Dec. 23, 1952. Added to the repertory of the New York City Ballet, New York, Oct. 1, 1964.

Pillar of Fire

Choreography: Antony Tudor; music: Arnold Schoenberg (Verklaerte Nacht); scenery and costumes: Jo Mielziner. First produced by Ballet Theatre (now the American Ballet Theatre), New York, Apr. 8, 1942.

Les Présages (Destinies)
Choreography: Leonide Massine; music: Tchaikovsky (Fifth Symphony); scenery and costumes: André Masson. First produced by the Ballet Russe de Monte Carlo at Monte Carlo, Apr. 13, 1933. Subsequently presented in America, New York, Dec. 22, 1933.

Prince Igor
Choreography: Michel Fokine; music: Alexander Borodin (Polovtsian Dances from the opera *Prince Igor*); scenery and costumes: Nicholas Roerich. First produced by Diaghileff's Ballets Russes, Paris, May 19, 1909. First presented in America by the same company, New York, Jan. 12, 1916. Revived by the Ballet Russe de Monte Carlo, New York, Jan. 10, 1934.

The Prodigal Son (Le Fils Prodigue)
Choreography: George Balanchine; music: Serge Prokofieff; scenery and costumes: Georges Rouault. First produced by Diaghileff's Ballets Russes, Paris, May 21, 1929. Revived by the New York City Ballet, New York, Feb. 23, 1950. Another version, with choreography by David Lichine, was produced by the Original Ballet Russe, Sydney, Australia, Dec. 1, 1939; New York, Nov. 26, 1940.

Prologue
Choreography: Jacques d'Amboise; music: William Byrd, Giles Farnaby and other 16th-century composers, selected and arranged by Robert Irving; scenery and costumes: Peter Larkin. First performance: New York, Jan. 12, 1967; New York City Ballet.

The Rake's Progress
Choreography: Ninette de Valois; music and book: Gavin Gordon; scenery and costumes: Rex Whistler. First produced by the Sadler's Wells Ballet (now the Royal Ballet), London, May 20, 1935. First presented in America by the same company, New York, Oct. 12, 1949.

Raymonda
Choreography: Marius Petipa; music: Alexander Glazounov; scenery and costumes: Allegri, Ivanov, Lambini. First produced by the Russian Imperial Ballet, Jan. 7 (Julian or Russian calendar) or Jan. 19 (Gregorian or Western calendar), 1898. Restaged for the Ballet Russe de Monte Carlo by Alexandra Danilova and George Balanchine, with scenery and costumes by Alexandre Benois, New York, Mar. 12, 1946. Extracts from *Raymonda* are frequently presented as a one-act divertissement ballet under the same title.

Raymonda Variations
Choreography: George Balanchine; music: Alexander Glazounov; scenery: Horace Armistead (backdrop for Lilac Garden): costumes:

Karinska. First presented by the New York City Ballet (under the title *Valses et Variations*), New York, Dec. 7, 1961.

Les Rendezvous
Choreography: Frederick Ashton; music: François Auber, arranged by Constant Lambert; scenery and costumes: William Chappell. First presented by the Sadler's Wells Ballet (now the Royal Ballet), London, Dec. 5, 1933. First presented in America by the Sadler's Wells Theatre Ballet, Minneapolis, Nov. 7, 1951 (New York, Mar. 25, 1952). Also in the repertory of the National Ballet of Canada.

Ricercare
Choreography: Glen Tetley; music: Mordecai Seter; setting: Rouben Ter-Artunian. First performance, Jan. 25, 1966, New York State Theater, American Ballet Theatre.

The Rite of Spring (See *Le Sacre du Printemps*)

Romeo and Juliet
Choreography: L. Lavrosky; music: Serge Prokofieff; scenery and costumes: Peter Williams. First produced by the Russian State Ballet, Leningrad, 1940; first performance at the Bolshoi Theater, Moscow, Dec. 28, 1946. First presented in America by the Bolshoi Ballet, New York City, Apr. 16, 1959. In three acts. Prior to the American presentation made into a full-length Russian motion picture in color, *The Ballet of Romeo and Juliet*. The story, in a one-act version, with choreography by Antony Tudor, music by Frederick Delius and scenery and costumes by Eugene Berman, was first produced by Ballet Theatre (now the American Ballet Theatre), New York, Apr. 6, 1943, in incomplete form. The finished work was presented Apr. 10 of the same year. Still another *Romeo and Juliet*, in three acts and eleven scenes, with choreography by Frederick Ashton, music by Prokofieff and scenery and costumes by Peter Rice, was produced by the Royal Danish Ballet in Copenhagen, May 19, 1955, and first presented in America in New York, Sept. 26, 1956. Choreography: Kenneth MacMillan; music: Serge Prokofieff; scenery and costumes: Nicholas Georgiadis. First presented by the Royal Ballet, London, Feb. 9, 1965. First presented in America by the same company, New York, Apr. 21, 1965. There are still other dance stagings—some elaborate productions, and some even in simplified *pas de deux* form.

Rouge et Noir
Choreography: Leonide Massine: music: Dmitri Shostakovitch (First Symphony); scenery and costumes: Henri Matisse. First produced by the Ballet Russe de Monte Carlo at Monte Carlo, May 11, 1939. First American performance by the same company, New York, Oct. 28, 1939.

Le Sacre du Printemps (The Rite of Spring)
Choreography: Vaslav Nijinsky; music: Igor Stravinsky; book: Stravinsky and Nicholas Roerich; scenery and costumes: Roerich. First produced by Diaghileff's Ballets Russes, Paris, May 29, 1913. Rechoreographed by Leonide Massine for the same company, Paris, 1920. Revised again by Massine in collaboration with Martha Graham (as leading dancer), Philadelphia, Apr. 11, 1930, under the auspices of the League of Composers. Restaged by Massine for the Royal Swedish Ballet, Stockholm, Apr. 30, 1956. The ballet has also been produced by other choreographers, among them a version with choreography by Kenneth MacMillan, with scenery and costumes by Sidney Nolan, presented by the Royal Ballet, London, May 3, 1962; first presented by the same company in the United States, New York, May 8, 1963. A Soviet version, with choreography by Natalia Kasatkina and Vladimir Vasiliov and scenery and costumes by A. D. Goncharov, was presented for the first time in America by the Bolshoi Ballet, New York, Apr. 26, 1966.

Saint Francis (Noblissima Visione)
Choreography: Leonide Massine; music: Paul Hindemith; book: Massine, Hindemith; scenery and costumes: Pavel Tchelitcheff. First produced by the Ballet Russe de Monte Carlo, London, July 21, 1938. First American performance, by the same company, New York, Oct. 14, 1938.

Scènes de Ballet
Choreography: Frederick Ashton; music: Igor Stravinsky; scenery and costumes: André Beaurepaire. First produced by the Sadler's Wells Ballet (now the Royal Ballet), London, Feb. 11, 1948. First presented in America by the same company, New York, Sept. 14, 1955. An earlier treatment, choreographed by Anton Dolin and featuring Dolin and Alicia Markova, was presented in the revue, *The Seven Lively Arts*, New York, Dec. 7, 1944.

Scheherazade
Choreography: Michel Fokine; music: Nicholas Rimsky-Korsakoff; book: Alexandre Benois, scenery and costumes: Léon Bakst. First produced by Diaghileff's Ballets Russes, Paris, June 4, 1910. A production unauthorized by the choreographer was presented during Gertrude Hoffman's *Saison Russe*, New York, June 14, 1911, in a staging by Theodore Kosloff. The Diaghileff company brought the authorized Fokine production to America in 1916. The Ballet Russe de Monte Carlo reintroduced the Fokine ballet to New York, Oct. 9, 1935, and it has remained in the repertory of this company ever since.

Scotch Symphony

Choreography: George Balanchine; music: Felix Mendelssohn (first movement of the Mendelssohn score is omitted); scenery: Horace Armistead; costumes: Karinska and David Ffolkes. First produced by the New York City Ballet, New York, Nov. 11, 1952. Added to the repertory of the City Center Joffrey Ballet, New York, Mar. 16, 1967.

Sea Shadow

Choreography: Gerald Arpino; music: Maurice Ravel; décor: Ming Cho Lee. First presented by the Robert Joffrey Ballet (now the City Center Joffrey Ballet) during the Rebekah Harkness Dance Festival, Central Park, New York, Sept. 5, 1963. Because of difficulties with the Ravel estate, a new score was commissioned by Michael Colgrass.

Sebastian

Choreography: Edward Caton; music: Gian-Carlo Menotti; scenery: Oliver Smith; costumes: Milena. First produced by the Ballet International, New York, Oct. 31, 1944. Restaged with wholly new choreography by Agnes de Mille for the American Ballet Theatre, New York, May 27, 1957 (in an initial workshop production).

Serenade

Choreography: George Balanchine; music: Tchaikovsky (Serenade in C Major for String Orchestra); costumes: Jean Lurcat. First presented by students of the School of American Ballet, White Plains, N.Y., June 10, 1934. Later presented by the American Ballet, New York, Mar. 1, 1935; by the Ballet Russe de Monte Carlo, New York, Oct. 17, 1940; by the American Ballet Caravan, 1941; by the Paris Opera Ballet, Paris, Apr. 30, 1947; by the New York City Ballet (with costumes by Karinska), New York, Oct. 18, 1948, by the Royal Danish Ballet, Copenhagen, 1957; by the Royal Ballet, May 7, 1967.

The Seven Deadly Sins

Choreography: George Balanchine; music: Kurt Weill; libretto: Berthold Brecht. First produced by Les Ballets, 1933, Paris, June 7, 1933. First produced in America by the New York City Ballet, with a new translation of the Brecht libretto by W. H. Auden and Chester Kallman and scenery and costumes by Rouben Ter-Artunian, New York, Dec. 4, 1958.

Seventh Symphony

Choreography: Leonide Massine; music: Beethoven; scenery and costumes: Christian Bérard. First produced by the Ballet Russe de Monte Carlo, Monte Carlo, May 5, 1938. First presented in America by the same company, New York, Oct. 15, 1938.

Shadowplay
    Choreography: Antony Tudor; music: Charles Koechlin; scenery and costumes: Michael Annals. First performed by the Royal Ballet, London, Jan. 25, 1967. First presented in America by the same company, New York, Apr. 29, 1967.

The Sleeping Beauty (La Belle au Bois Dormant)
    Choreography: Marius Petipa; music: Tchaikovsky; book by Petipa and Ivan Vsevolojsky, after tales by Charles Perrault; scenery and costumes: Vsevolojsky. First produced by the Russian Imperial Ballet, St. Petersburg, Jan. 3 (Julian or Russian calendar) or Jan. 15 (Gregorian or Western calendar), 1890. First presented in Western Europe by Diaghileff's Ballets Russes, staged by Nicholas Sergeyev, with additional choreography by Bronislava Nijinska and scenery and costumes by Léon Bakst, London, Nov. 2, 1921. First presented in America by the Philadelphia Ballet, with choreography by Catherine Littlefield, Philadelphia, Feb. 11, 1937. Staged by the Sadler's Wells Ballet (now the Royal Ballet) under the supervision of Sergeyev and with scenery and costumes by Nadia Benois, London, Feb. 2, 1939; restaged by the same company in a new production, with additional choreography by Frederick Ashton and Ninette de Valois and with scenery and costumes by Oliver Messel, Feb. 20, 1946; presented in America by the same company, New York, Oct. 9, 1949. Produced by the Royal Danish Ballet, with direction by Ninette de Valois and scenery and costumes by André Delfau, Copenhagen, 1957.

Solitaire
    Choreography: Kenneth MacMillan; music: Malcolm Arnold; décor and costumes: Desmond Heeley. First produced by the Sadler's Wells Theatre Ballet, London, June 7, 1956. Later added to the repertory of the Sadler's Wells Ballet (now the Royal Ballet). First presented in America by the Royal Ballet, New York, Sept. 17, 1957.

Song of the Earth
    Choreography: Kenneth MacMillan; music: Gustav Mahler (Das Lied von der Erde). First presented by the Royal Ballet, London, May 19, 1966; performed by the same company for the first time in America, New York, Apr. 25, 1967.

Le Spectre de la Rose (The Spirit of the Rose)
    Choreography: Michel Fokine; music: Carl Maria von Weber (Invitation to the Dance); book: J. L. Vaudoyer; scenery and costumes: Léon Bakst. First produced by Diaghileff's Ballets Russes, Monte Carlo, Apr. 19, 1911. First presented in America by the same company, New York, Apr. 3, 1916. Added to the repertory of the Ballet Russe de Monte Carlo and other companies.

Square Dance
Choreography: George Balanchine; music: Corelli (excerpts, Suite for Strings) and Vivaldi (excerpts, Concerti Grossi). First presented by the New York City Ballet, New York, Nov. 21, 1957.

Stars and Stripes
Choreography: George Balanchine; music: John Philip Sousa (arranged and orchestrated by Hershy Kay); scenery: David Hays; costumes: Karinska. First produced by the New York City Ballet, New York, Jan. 17, 1958.

The Still Point
Choreography: Todd Bolender; music: Claude Debussy (String Quartet, transcribed for orchestra by Frank Black). First presented in ballet repertory by the New York City Ballet, New York, Mar. 13, 1956. (An earlier version, staged by Bolender for the Dance Drama Company, a modern dance group headed by Emily Frankel and Mark Ryder, had its première Aug. 3, 1955, at the Jacob's Pillow Dance Festival at Lee, Mass.)

The Stone Flower
Choreography: Yuri Grigorovich; music: Serge Prokofieff; libretto: Mirra Prokofieva (based on a story by Pavel Bazhov); scenery and costumes: Simon Versaladze. First presented in Leningrad by the Bolshoi Ballet, July 6, 1958, and in Moscow, Mar. 7, 1959. (An earlier version was given at the Bolshoi Theatre in Moscow, Feb. 12, 1954). First presented by the Bolshoi Ballet in New York, May 4, 1959.

A Streetcar Named Desire
Choreography: Valerie Bettis; music: Alex North, orchestrated by Rayburn Wright; scenery: Peter Larkin; costumes: Saul Bolasni; based upon the play of the same name by Tennessee Williams. First produced by the Slavenska-Franklin Ballet, Montreal, Oct. 9, 1952. First presented in New York by the same company, Dec. 8, 1952. Added to the repertory of Ballet Theatre (now the American Ballet Theatre), Princeton, Oct. 26, 1954.

Swan Lake (Le Lac des Cygnes)
Choreography (in first staging): Julius Reisinger; music: Tchaikovsky; book: V. P. Begitchev and Vasily Geltzer. First produced by the Russian Imperial Ballet, Moscow, Feb. 20 (Julian or Russian calendar) or Mar. 4 (Gregorian or Western calendar), 1877. Reproduced by the Russian Imperial Ballet, with wholly new choreography by Marius Petipa and Lev Ivanov and scenery by Botcharov and Levogt, St. Petersburg, Jan. 5 (Julian calendar) or Jan. 17 (Gregorian calendar), 1895. First presented in America in a production staged by Mikhail Mordkin, with scenery by James Fox and

performed by a company headed by Catherine Geltzer and Mordkin, New York, Dec. 19, 1911. First presented in full-length form in England by the Sadler's Wells Ballet (now the Royal Ballet), with the Petipa-Ivanov choreography re-created by Nicholas Sergeyev and scenery and costumes by Hugh Stevenson, London, Nov. 20, 1934: revived by the same company, with new settings and costumes by Leslie Hurry, Sept. 7, 1943; new productions followed, with same designer, in 1948 and 1952; first given in America by the same company, New York, Oct. 20, 1949. The most recent Royal Ballet version, with choreography credited to Frederick Ashton, Rudolph Nureyev and Maria Fay, and with scenery and costumes by Carl Toms, was first presented in London, Dec. 12, 1963; first presented in America by the same company, New York, May 6, 1965. The Bolshoi Ballet's current four-act production has choreography by Alexander Gorsky (Acts I, II, III) and Asaf Messerer (Act IV), with subsequent revisions by Messerer and Alexander Radunsky and scenery and costumes by Simon Versaladze; first presented in New York, Apr. 21, 1959. The San Francisco Ballet also produced a full-length *Swan Lake* in San Francisco, 1940, with choreography by Lew Christensen. A full-length *Swan Lake* was added to the repertory of the American Ballet Theatre, with choreography by David Blair (after Petipa and Ivanov), scenery by Oliver Smith, and costumes by Freddy Wittop, Chicago, Feb. 16, 1967; the first New York performance, May 9, 1967 (Act II was presented alone in New York, Jan. 18, 1966). *Swan Lake* in one-act form (Act II of the original) was presented in St. Petersburg, Feb. 29, 1894, with choreography by Ivanov (one year before the full Petipa-Ivanov ballet was presented). In one-act form (Act II), *Swan Lake* is in the repertory of many ballet organizations: the Ballet Russe de Monte Carlo, the New York City Ballet and others. The New York City Ballet's *Swan Lake*, with choreography by George Balanchine, was first presented in New York, Nov. 20, 1951.

La Sylphide

Choreography: Philippe Taglioni; music: Jean Schnitzhoeffer; book: Adolphe Nourrit; scenery: Pierre Ciceri; costumes: Eugène Lami. First presented in Paris, Mar. 12, 1832. Presented in London, July 26, 1832; in St. Petersburg, Sept. 18, 1837; Milan, May 29, 1841 (all with Marie Taglioni, who created the title role). An earlier St. Petersburg presentation, with Croisette as the ballerina, took place May 28 (Julian or Russian calendar) or June 9 (Gregorian or Western calendar), 1835. First presented in America in an adapted version, New York, Apr. 15, 1835. Produced by the Royal Danish Ballet, with choreography by August Bournonville and music by

Herman Lovenskjold and scenery by Christian Petersen, Copenhagen, Nov. 28, 1836 (has remained continously in the Danish repertory). Produced by Harald Lander (after Bournonville), with music by Edgar Cosma (after Lovenskjold) and scenery and costumes by Robert O'Hearn, for the American Ballet Theatre, New York, Mar. 13, 1965. Taglioni ballet revived, with choreography by Victor Gsovsky, scenery by Serebriakov, and costumes by Christian Bérard by the Ballets des Champs-Elysées, Paris, Dec. 1946. The first-known ballet by this title was given in Milan, May 28, 1828, with choreography by Luigi Henry, music by Carlini and with (probably) Teresa Heberle as the ballerina.

Les Sylphides (See also *Chopiniana*)

Choreography: Michel Fokine; music: Frédéric Chopin; scenery and costumes: Alexandre Benois. First produced by Diaghileff's Ballets Russes, Paris, June 2, 1909. An earlier version by Fokine, called *Chopiniana* and danced by members of the Russian Imperial Ballet, was first presented in St. Petersburg, Mar. 21, 1908. First performed in America by the Diaghileff company, New York, Jan. 20, 1916 (an unauthorized version had been given by Gertrude Hoffman in New York, June 10, 1911). Added to the repertories of the following major companies: Royal Danish Ballet, Copenhagen, Oct. 14, 1925; Ballet Russe de Monte Carlo, Jan. 10, 1934; Ballet Theatre (now the American Ballet Theatre), New York, Jan. 11, 1940; the Sadler's Wells Ballet (now the Royal Ballet), London, Mar. 8, 1932; the Sadler's Wells Theatre Ballet, Apr. 22, 1946; also other companies and ensembles. The Royal Danish Ballet's production, staged by Fokine himself, is called *Chopiniana* and this title is occasionally used by other companies, among them the Bolshoi Ballet.

Sylvia

Choreography: Louis Mérante; music: Léo Delibes; book: Jules Barbier and Baron de Reinach; scenery: Chéret, Rubé, Chaperon; costumes: Lacoste. (Rita Sangalli was the first Sylvia.) First produced by the Paris Opera, Paris, June 14, 1876. Revived by the same institution and restaged by Leo Staats, Dec. 19, 1919; by Serge Lifar, Feb. 12, 1941; by Albert Aveline, 1946. First presented in St. Petersburg by the Russian Imperial Ballet, Dec. 2 (Julian or Russian calendar) or Dec. 15 (Gregorian or Western calendar), 1901, with Olga Preobrajenska in the title part. Produced by the Sadler's Wells Ballet (now the Royal Ballet), with entirely new choreography by Frederick Ashton and with scenery and costumes by Robin and Christopher Ironside, London, Sept. 3, 1952; first presented by the same company in America, New York, Sept. 29, 1953.

Sylvia Pas de Deux
Choreography: George Balanchine; music: Léo Delibes; costumes: Karinska. First produced by the New York City Ballet, New York, Dec. 1, 1950.

Symphonic Variations
Choreography: Frederick Ashton; music: César Franck; scenery and costumes: Sophie Fedorovitch. First produced by the Sadler's Wells Ballet (now the Royal Ballet), London, Apr. 24, 1946. First presented in America by the same company, New York, Oct. 12, 1949.

Symphonie Concertante
Choreography: George Balanchine; music: Wolfgang Amadeus Mozart (Sinfonia Concertante in E flat major for Violin and Viola); scenery and costumes: James Stewart Morcom. First presented by the New York City Ballet, New York, Nov. 12, 1947. (At that time, the New York City Ballet was known as the Ballet Society.)

Symphonie Fantastique
Choreography: Leonide Massine; music (and storyline): Hector Berlioz; scenery and costumes: Christian Bérard. First produced by the Ballet Russe de Monte Carlo, London, July 24, 1936. First presented in America by the same company, New York, Oct. 29, 1936.

Symphony in C
Choreography: George Balanchine; music: Georges Bizet. First produced as *Le Palais de Crystal,* with scenery and costumes by Léonor Fini, by the Paris Opera Ballet, Paris, July 28, 1947. First presented in America as *A Symphony in C* by the Ballet Society (now the New York City Ballet), New York, Mar. 22, 1948. Added to the repertory of the Royal Danish Ballet, Copenhagen, Oct. 4, 1952.

Tally-Ho! (or *The Frail Quarry*)
Choreography: Agnes de Mille; music: Christoph Gluck, arranged by Paul Nordoff; scenery and costumes: Motley. First produced by Ballet Theatre (now the American Ballet Theatre), Los Angeles, Feb. 25, 1944.

Theme and Variations
Choreography: George Balanchine; music: Tchaikovsky (final movement of Suite No. 3 in G); scenery and costumes: Woodman Thompson. First produced by Ballet Theatre, New York, Nov. 26, 1947, and by the New York City Ballet, New York, Feb. 5, 1966.

The Three-Cornered Hat (Le Tricorne)
Choreography: Leonide Massine; music: Manuel de Falla; book:

Martinez Sierra; scenery and costumes: Pablo Picasso. First produced by Diaghileff's Ballets Russes, London, July 22, 1919. First presented in America by the Ballet Russe de Monte Carlo, New York, Mar. 9, 1934. The ballet is also in the repertories of the American Ballet Theatre, the Royal Ballet (Sadler's Wells), the Royal Swedish Ballet and other companies.

Three Virgins and a Devil

Choreography: Agnes de Mille; music: Ottorino Respighi; scenario: Ramon Reed; scenery: Arne Lundborg; costumes: Motley. First produced by Ballet Theatre (now the American Ballet Theatre), New York, Feb. 11, 1941. (An earlier version of the ballet, using different music, was seen in a London revue in 1934.)

Undertow

Choreography: Antony Tudor; music: William Schuman; libretto: Tudor, after a suggestion by John van Druten; scenery and costumes: Raymond Breinin. First produced by Ballet Theatre (now the American Ballet Theatre), New York, Apr. 10, 1945.

La Valse

Choreography: George Balanchine; music: Maurice Ravel (Valses Nobles et Sentimentales and La Valse); costumes: Karinska. First produced by the New York City Ballet, New York, Feb. 20, 1951. Another version, with entirely different choreography by Frederick Ashton, was presented by the La Scala Opera Ballet, Milan, Feb. 1, 1958. First presented by the Royal Ballet, with costumes by André Levasseur, London, Mar. 10, 1959.

Variations

Choreography: George Balanchine; music: Igor Stravinsky (Variations in memory of Aldous Huxley). First presented by the New York City Ballet, New York, Mar. 31, 1966.

Variations for Four

Choreography: Anton Dolin; music: Marguerite Keogh; costumes: Tom Lingwood. First presented by the London Festival Ballet, London, Sept. 5, 1957. First American presentation, the Ed Sullivan Show, CBS-TV, Mar. 30, 1958; first American stage presentation, American Ballet Theatre, Sept. 25, 1958.

La Ventana

Choreography: August Bournonville; music: H. C. Lumbye. First produced by the Royal Danish Ballet, Copenhagen, 1854 (an earlier and somewhat different version was created by Bournonville for a recital performance in a casino). Revised by the choreographer in 1856. Revised by Frank Schaufuss and Hans Brenaa in 1956. First presented in America, Oct. 28, 1956, in Brooklyn, during the United States tour of the Royal Danish Ballet.

Viva Vivaldi
Choreography: Gerald Arpino; music: Antonio Vivaldi, adapted from his Violin Concerto, P. 151, by Rodrigo Riera. First performed by the Robert Joffrey Ballet (now the City Center Joffrey Ballet), at the Rebekah Harkness Dance Festival, Central Park, N.Y., Sept. 11, 1965.

A Wedding Bouquet
Choreography: Frederick Ashton; music, scenery and costumes: Lord Berners; words: Gertrude Stein. First produced by the Vic-Wells Ballet (later the Sadler's Wells Ballet and now the Royal Ballet), Apr. 27, 1937, London. First American performance by the same company, New York, Oct. 25, 1949.

Western Symphony
Choreography: George Balanchine; music: Hershy Kay (symphony based on American folk themes); scenery by John Boyt and costumes by Karinska added Feb. 27, 1955. First produced, without formal scenery and costumes, by the New York City Ballet, New York, Sept. 7, 1954.

The Whims of Cupid and the Ballet Master
Choreography: Vincenzo Galeotti; music: Jens Lolle. First produced by the Royal Danish Ballet, Copenhagen, 1786. First presented in America by the Royal Danish Ballet, New York, Sept. 22, 1956.

Index

J
i